A HANDBOOK FOR PARENTS AND EDUCATORS TO PROMOTE
POSITIVE CHANGE BASED ON THE PRINCIPLES OF MINDFULNESS

ROOTS AND WINGS

CHILDHOOD NEEDS A REVOLUTION

ALEX KOSTER M.Ed.

ROOTS AND WINGS

First published by Roots & Wings Publishing
Clonmel
Tipperary
Ireland
www.rootsandwings.pub
email: alex@rootsandwings.pub

Paperback	ISBN: 978-1-78846-031-6
Ebook – mobi format	ISBN: 978-1-78846-032-3
Ebook – ePub format	ISBN: 978-1-78846-033-0
CreateSpace	ISBN: 978-1-78846-034-7

Disclaimer:

This book was written to provide information and motivation to the reader. It is sold with the understanding that the author is not engaged to render any type of psychological or other kind of professional advice. The content of each chapter is based on the personal opinion, professional knowledge and experience of the author underpinned by consulting the opinions of renowned researchers in their own fields of expertise. This book is in no way intended to be used as a programme to prevent or cure mental health issues and you should always consult a health professional should you have concerns about your own or your child's mental or physical well-being. The author shall not be liable for any damages, including, but not limited to, special, incidental, consequential or other damages. The reader shall be responsible for his/her choices, actions, and results.

A CIP catalogue record for this book is
available from the British Library

Produced by Kazoo Independent Publishing Services
222 Beech Park, Lucan, Co. Dublin
www.kazoopublishing.com

Kazoo Independent Publishing Services is not the publisher of this work. All rights and responsibilities pertaining to this work remain with Roots & Wings Publishing.

Cover illustration by Cathy Dineen
Cover design by Andrew Brown

Printed in the EU

Permissions

Alits, Berit. photography

Asmussen, Dan. Story on his facebook page 21.07.2015.

Bergstrom, Chris. (2016) The Mindful Brain – Mindfulness and the brain – How to explain it to children. http://blissfulkids.com/mindfulness-and-the-brain-how-to-explain-it-to-children/

Berry, Lucy. Poem "The Last Time" http://www.lucyberry.com/

Brensilver, Matthew. (2016) What is Mindfulness? http://www.mindfulschools.org/foundational-concepts/what-is-mindfulness/

Burdick, Debra. (2014) *Mindfulness skills for kids and teens*. Eau Claire, PESI Publishing & Media.

Ekman, Paul (Dr) and Ekman, Eve (Dr). The Atlas of Emotions. www.atlasofemotions.org

Kabat-Zinn, Myla and Kabat-Zinn, Jon (Dr.). (2014) *Everyday Blessings – The Inner Work of Mindful Parenting*. London, Piatkus.

Kernan, Margaret (Ph D). (2007) Play as a context for Early Learning and Development – A research paper. Dublin, NCCA.

Neff, Kristin (Dr). (2017) What is Self-Compassion? http://self-compassion.org/the-three-elements-of-self-compassion-2/

Roeper, Malte. (2011) *Kinder raus!* Muenchen, Suedwest Verlag.

Siegel, Daniel (Dr). (2014) *Brainstorm*. London, Scribe Publications.

Siegel, Daniel (Dr). (2010) *Mindsight: Transform Your Brain with the New Science of Kindness*. New York, Bantam Books.

Siegel, Daniel (Dr).; Payne Bryson, T. (2012) *The Whole Brain Child*. New York, Bantam Books.

Snel, Eline. (2013) *Sitting still like a Frog*. Boston, Shambala Publications.

Contents

PART 2

"Give the ones you love wings to fly, roots to come back and reasons to stay."

DALAI LAMA

Introduction

It is easier to raise happy children than to repair
broken adults

Hello and welcome to this book. If you are reading this, you are likely interested in how we can make positive changes for ourselves and our children in navigating the challenging times we live in. I invite you to explore these challenges with me and find ways and ideas to raise happy and compassionate children despite these difficulties. In order to be available and present for our children, our families and ourselves, it is equally important that we take care of ourselves as parents and educators in the process. We all know the saying "your health is your wealth", and that goes for both physical and mental health. As someone who has her own mental health challenges caused both by a genetic condition (sensory processing sensitivity), as well as personal circumstances, I know the detrimental effects these have on emotional well-being and enjoyment of life in general. I was very lucky to have been introduced to mindfulness many years ago, and even though I still struggle with anxiety, worry and stress-related symptoms at times, mindfulness has given me invaluable tools to deal with these issues and make the necessary lifestyle changes. The study of mindfulness and its scientific basis has helped me to come to an understanding of the physiological processes involved and has reinforced my passion for advocating a mindful lifestyle.

I believe that we, as a society, need to move away from today's fast-paced, competitive and self-centred outlook and move towards more compassion, integration, kindness and connectedness. We need to go back to basics in many areas of our lives. I'm aware this might sound very naïve, but please bear with me. There are reasons beyond the obvious, which I will explain in more detail in the following chapters. Although I am a teacher, a mum to two young daughters (both of whom present with anxiety-related issues, and the oldest girl is also diagnosed with ASD) and I have practised and studied mindfulness for some years now, I wouldn't expect you to wholly rely on my ideas and theories, so I have consulted many experts and their scientific research to back up my personal views and ideas.

I wrote this book for us mums and dads, who love our children to the moon and back. We would do anything to "make" them happy, and we worry about their ability to cope with modern-day challenges. I also wrote this book for us educators, as I believe we need to adjust our approach to education in order to respond to current issues and prioritise our students' well-being and the learning of essential life skills over a mostly academic and competitive focus. This book is also intended for coaches, caregivers and anybody who is involved in children's lives and has an interest in building a positive future for our society.

Being a parent is one of the most important and diverse "professions" in the world. We are carers, educators, nurses, chefs, taxi drivers, entertainers, counsellors, storytellers, tear-dryers, goodnight-kissers and much more. We're supposed to know what to do in every situation life throws at us because we're the "grown-ups" after all! That sounds pretty exciting but also very challenging and even frightening at times, don't you think? Nobody handed us certificates of qualification when we first became parents. There were no diplomas, no degrees and no job interviews; we were just thrown into the cold deep water, some waters colder than others. When you add difficult contemporary conditions and phenomena to this sense of being unprepared, it is no wonder we can feel overwhelmed, scared and helpless sometimes, both for ourselves and for our children. Children in today's society are growing up in very different circumstances than we or our parents did. The many challenges experienced by parents, educators and by our children can push us all to our very limits. That is why I passionately believe a mindful lifestyle, with all that entails, could be an invaluable support for any family to bring more presence, peace, stability, joy and "togetherness" to our interactions, our homes and beyond.

Mindfulness to me is so much more than simply meditation

practice; it's a way of life. Whether you know it or not, you are already practising mindfulness every day, maybe just for a few seconds or a couple of minutes. It could be while tasting the first sip of your morning coffee, smelling the delicious scent of a home-cooked dinner, feeling the touch of your child's hand or enjoying the sea breeze while walking along the beach – all of these are mindful moments: moments when we are consciously paying attention and being present.

I strongly believe that the early introduction of a mindful attitude and approach to life can make a big difference to our children's and our own lives. It can greatly contribute to secure and harmonious connections within families and communities, and provide invaluable life skills to handle the challenges that life will bring. Mindful living can enhance happiness, well-being and the simple enjoyment of our lives, as we pay attention to what is important and already here rather than continuously chasing faraway dreams. Of course everybody should have goals to strive towards and dreams they want to achieve in their lifetime. The problem is that oftentimes we miss many of the beautiful things along the way and lose sight of the incredible people and occurrences that are already enriching our lives in this very moment. Including a mindful attitude into our daily interactions will help us and our children to stop and pause, look around, smile every so often and appreciate the gifts and blessings around us. It will help us manage challenges and make good and balanced choices rather than reacting mindlessly, creating situations that we might regret a second later.

The catalyst for writing this book was a feeling of helplessness, frustration, anger, sadness and even outrage. I know it might sound a little odd to start a book based on the principles of mindfulness with quite a pessimistic statement, but please bear with me. These feelings have popped up again and again in recent years whenever I thought about or observed how children grow up in our modern Western society. I overheard a conversation recently in a restaurant, a part of which I couldn't get out of my head: "Children nowadays don't know how lucky they are. There has never been a better time to grow up in!" I was incredulous. I want to be careful about generalising too much because life, even in our modern Western society, is not the same for every family; far from it. I understand where these elderly people were coming from. Of course there are many things that have changed in the last fifty years that we ought to be very grateful for. Children have not had to experience war, healthcare has improved dramatically, most families can provide some degree of financial stability and every child has access to education. Children have opportunities like never before: foreign travel, technology and information at the click of a button and access to a wide range of leisure activities and hobbies. But do we really believe that children nowadays are better off than children thirty or forty years ago? Do we think childhood and raising children is a walk in the park compared to our own or our parents' upbringing? I very much doubt it.

Children may have more wealth in a materialistic sense, but I believe that core values are being eroded more and more. There is a significant rise in mental health issues at an early age, which is starting to manifest in our current generation of teenagers. These mental health issues are transpiring in trends such as the rise of teenage and child suicide, anxiety and depression, intimidation and bullying behaviours. Consequently, teenagers experience disturbing violent actions and a lack of respect for themselves and others; the latter frequently results in a warped unrealistic body image and inappropriate sexual behaviours to mention just a few examples.

We can blame some of this on the media, technology and social media. Magazines, adverts, movies, websites and television shows portray unrealistic images of what we should look like. Beauty is defined as being flawless, perfect and sterile with little wriggle room. Widespread availability of smartphones and ever-present access to the internet facilitates easy access to pornography, violent games and movies, questionable chatrooms and social media outlets. In series five, episode one of the Channel 4 programme *The Sex Education Show*, parents in a high school were invited to a "screening" in a cinema. They were shown a selection of video material compiled from data collected via an anonymous poll the children had participated in, which revealed what they had seen or accessed online in relation to porn and violence. The viewer did not see the content; they only saw the parents' reactions when shown the film. These reactions included crying, vomiting, screaming and running out of the cinema, all of which clearly indicated the severe and graphic content of the film. One researcher had even refused to continue investigating because the content was too disturbing. As a parent, the issues around internet access and inappropriate content is the biggest fear I have for my children's future.

Some issues are and always have been just part of growing up: peer pressure, competition in school and sports and finding our own place within ourselves and our environment. It is necessary that children overcome obstacles independently in order to grow and develop. But we also need to address our own responsibilities: the way we educate and raise our children and what we can do to equip our children with skills they need to overcome such obstacles.

Following countless discussions throughout the years with friends, family and colleagues, I know that I am not alone in my sentiment. Even though I might sound pessimistic, I passionately believe we can all contribute towards helping our children grow up to be responsible, strong, content, kind-hearted adults. All members of society – parents, educators, family members, neighbours, friends, politicians – can make it happen. It doesn't take a radical immediate overhaul of our lives; we can start by making small simple changes. With this book I want to encourage you to believe that we can all make a change to help the most vulnerable members of our society feel loved and valued, gain self-worth and confidence, have compassion towards themselves and others and be able to lead happy lives. Everybody wants the best for their children, for them to have a good childhood and grow up in an inclusive and supportive society.

The idea for writing this book has grown gradually over the years and stems from my personal family history, my experience as a teacher, personal mindfulness practice and research in this area, and it got its final push when I became a mother myself. Throughout the years, I have read many books and articles that dealt with certain elements of my ideas. They were like pieces of a jigsaw that began to fit together. One day I decided to start putting my thoughts on paper. It was a long process with many lulls, but I persevered, convinced of the importance and power of a mindful approach to everyday life, specifically in relation to parenting and raising children. Early intervention will plant the seed from a young age and contribute to a natural integration of a mindful lifestyle. As you will see later on, this doesn't necessarily require a structured and guided daily mindfulness or meditation regime, even though this can be of great benefit for your own well-being and I would recommend it as a foundation for a more informal approach.

To quote Dr Daniel J. Siegel and Mary Hartzell from their wonderful book, *Parenting from the Inside Out:* "This is not a how-to book – it is a how-we book." Sometimes books about parenting or education can make parents and educators feel inadequate, that we are doing something wrong and are not succeeding. My intention with this book could not be further from that. To be honest with you, as I was writing this book, the experience felt as if I was creating a kind of compass for my own parenting and teaching journey, to remind myself of the things that truly matter to me, to try and be the best parent and teacher I could be, with all my failings and downfalls. We all have busy lives, and I am as guilty as anyone else of sometimes using the television as a babysitter, of losing my temper and raising my voice, of my mind being full of things I need to get done while my three-year-old is trying to talk to me. That's just life.

I wanted this book to provide some tools and ideas to help us do the following:

- to integrate more mindfulness, even just mindful moments of being present, into our family interactions and encounters with both children and adults

- to be able to pull ourselves back into the here and now when our minds rush ahead

- to consciously make time for connecting with our children, with ourselves, our families and the world we live in

- to enjoy life with all that it has in store for us

- to be able to cope better in difficult and stressful situations.

If this book can help you to achieve a little bit of this then it was worthwhile. For ease of use I have divided the book into two sections: a "reading part" where I will give some personal and research-based insight into the different sub-topics, and a "practical part" where you will find some suggestions for exercises, activities, resources and templates to include into your everyday interactions or lesson plans.

In mindfulness meditation there are formal and informal meditation practices. Formal practice gives us a good starting point to live and act mindfully ourselves and as a result helps us to approach our children in a more mindful way. However, in this book, I concentrate more on informal exercises and approaches that can be easily integrated into everyday situations at home, in school or any other environment that involve the care and instruction of children.

Many activities are simply based on paying attention, on being present in the moment i.e. really listening and responding to children, being aware of our own emotional situation, pausing before we react and being mindful of how we interact with our children or anybody else for that matter. Some of these approaches don't really have anything to do with meditation as such, but sometimes we just need to make small changes to our environment or automated behaviours in order to create a space or positive change. From a child's perspective, exercises and activities should be short, motivating and meaningful in order for them to be naturally and easily integrated into their daily lives over time.

In the following chapters I will take a closer look at different areas of interest and concern and how we can make subtle and easily implemented adjustments that can have a positive impact. In the practical part, I will include specific exercises, which are mostly play based, that can be integrated in a fun way into daily life either at home or in any other child-centred environment.

Mindfulness meditation and exercises are important life skills that children should learn from an early age in order to internalise them and use them instinctively to deal with life's challenges. Adults and children alike will benefit from this mindful approach to everyday life.

Part 1

Chapter 1

It takes a village to raise a child

Today, more than ever, it is important that we all take collective responsibility for the children in our communities, whether they are our own or not. Family structures and society have changed considerably in the past twenty to thirty years, and factors like immigration, emigration, lifestyle changes and economic issues have had a severe impact on how children are raised. Years ago, it was a regular occurrence that multiple generations lived under one roof and helped to raise the children within the family unit. Other family members often lived close by and acted as an important support network. This supportive system is often missing in modern families due to the above-mentioned reasons. It's not just parents and families that raise a child. Everybody involved in children's daily lives has a responsibility to positively support, encourage, protect and encounter them with care and kindness. The "village" is as important today as ever.

Recently, I was confronted with a situation that could have potentially ended badly. I was in a lift in the shopping centre, and when the doors opened a gorgeous little girl of maybe one and a half years old was standing in front of me. She gave me a beautiful smile and a wave and tried to walk past me into the open lift. Her mum was nowhere to be seen, and this little girl could have easily got lost, hurt or at best become very frightened. I stayed with her and kept a lookout for her mum who came around the corner a minute later. She was about eight months pregnant and trying to keep up with her very sociable little daughter. Things happen so easily without any ill intentions or negligence. As parents, we have all had close calls; I know I have.

Our children spend a vast amount of their daily lives in the care of others, especially once they start school. It is our obligation to be involved in and informed about how they spend their time and if their needs are being met. Schools have an especially important influence in the raising and education of children, and even though I am a teacher myself, and I might be getting myself into hot water here, priorities, particularly in primary schools, are by no means child-centred enough. In my opinion, children start school at much too young an age in Ireland and other European countries. Developmentally speaking, they should still be able to just be children. Four- and five-year-old children want to play, run around and use their creativity and imagination. At that age emphasis should be placed on providing opportunities for movement, play and learning to socialise appropriately, not on how to sit still, listen to the teacher and carry out repetitive formal exercises.

Too much emphasis is put on academia and filling in and finishing books and copies. Writing and number work are often repetitive exercises that are not meaningful and end up being boring and frustrating for young children who naturally have an urge to move around, play and explore. Particularly children with additional learning needs experience a sense of failure, the feeling of not being good enough or as good as the others. This is because integration and differentiation for individual needs are still often just a physical exercise. Children with special needs might be attending a mainstream class, however, due to what I believe is an outdated system, large class sizes, staffing issues and a lack of resources, needs are met in a way that often makes it even more obvious that this child is different. If true differentiation, integration and a more general, flexible approach was employed in schools, children would be able to learn according to their own learning style.

Young children are very creative and this creativity is stifled very early on by regimented activities that hardly give any room for free expression. Art activities are often pre-cut, pre-drawn or have to be done under strict instructions with a certain outcome in mind. When "necessary", these activities are finished by the teacher in order for everybody to move on and be at the same level. I am not criticising schools or teachers. They are doing a fantastic job within a system and framework that puts certain demands and results at the forefront, prioritising them over what I believe to be more important: raising responsible, independent and compassionate children while incorporating essential learning content. When you are a teacher in a class of thirty pupils within the current system, choices are limited if you want to fulfil the demands and adhere to policies and guidelines. I will explore the possibilities schools should be able to afford our children in a little more detail later and encourage you, both as parents and educators, to get involved. Only if we voice our concerns to the people responsible can we be part of a positive change. There are many great initiatives on a national and local level introducing very worthwhile programmes in primary and secondary schools. These include healthy-eating impulses, mindfulness, yoga, art competitions and many more. The trouble is that these initiatives, as important as they are, end up being just drops on a hot stone and are usually limited in time. The education system needs a revamp from the bottom up, in which all these current efforts and programmes are imbedded as a priority, not as an add-on.

HAPPINESS

I can fully understand that some of you might pick up this book, roll your eyes up to heaven and mumble: "Seriously? Another book on mindfulness?" Phrases like "being present in the moment," "staying with your breath," "accept what is in this moment" are starting to sound tired and repetitive. There are endless publications on mindfulness, happiness, relaxation, wellness, well-being, yoga, Ayurveda, meditation etc. Radio programmes and television segments cover topics around these issues non-stop. Yes, I agree that many phrases are currently overused and are growing tired, but there must be a reason beyond just fashion for this phenomenon.

I believe that at the core lies happiness or the lack thereof. In a nutshell and very generally speaking, isn't happiness what all of us want for our children, our families, our friends and ourselves? But what is happiness? Webster's Online Dictionary offers the following definitions of happiness: *1) good fortune: prosperity; 2a) a state of well-being and contentment: joy; 2b) a pleasurable or satisfying experience.*

I will not go into the scientific approach of what happiness is: whether it is measurable or what the parameters may be. If anyone is interested in this, I can highly recommend books such as Martin E. Seligman's *Authentic Happiness*, Tal Ben-Shahar's *Happier* and Derren Brown's *Happy*. I will adopt a more general approach, as it's basically the reason why I am writing this book – to document my views on how we can contribute to raising happy children.

Happiness is a term that is influenced and defined by many varied factors and can mean different things to every individual. For his movie *Happiness is*, the director Andrew Shapter asked people for their definition of happiness. Answers ranged from "wading in the ocean", "being your children's bestest hero", "good health and looking at my kid while she is asleep" to "that feeling you get after you have selflessly helped someone who needed it" and "the smell of my grandpa's farm".

Happiness is defined by many factors: where you live in the world, personal preferences, cultural background, religious belief, life circumstances and much more. I can imagine that happiness for a mother in some parts of Africa is simply being able to provide clean water and enough food for her children, whereas a busy working dad in a European country would describe happiness as being able to spend some peaceful days with his family.

Meik Wiking, the CEO of the Happiness Research Institute in Copenhagen, writes in his book, *The Little Book of Hygge – The Danish Way to Live Well*: "Danes are the happiest people in Europe according to the European Social Survey, but they are also the ones who meet most often with their friends and family and feel the calmest and most peaceful".

In *Happier*, Tal Ben-Shahar defines happiness as the "overall experience of pleasure and meaning. A happy person enjoys positive emotions while perceiving her life as purposeful." I do like this explanation very much as it doesn't, as Ben-Shahar says himself, reduce happiness to single moments but expands the concept of happiness to one's overall experiences, meaning that even though we will experience painful episodes in our lives, we can still be a happy person if purpose and meaning are present.

To me personally, it appears that a mindful approach to parenting and raising children in a loving and secure home, in whichever form that may be, can be a good foundation for leading a happy and contented life. Of course this is a very general statement. Nobody knows what the future holds and what troubles and misfortunes, or indeed good fortune and luck, will come our way, but if we have firm roots and a supportive and loving network we will be able to weather the storms with more strength and ease. In the following chapters I want to try and give some guidance and ideas for providing this foundation for our children. Of course this is only a framework that could help you to integrate a more mindful approach into family life and beyond. You are the parent, you know your child best. These are just general ideas and you can tailor them to your own needs and beliefs. Like I said before, happiness comes in different shapes and sizes, just as our families do.

Chapter 2

The child within

It is often underestimated how much we are influenced by our childhood experiences. Even though it is known that childhood trauma such as child sexual abuse, domestic violence, death of a parent and other major traumatic events greatly influence a person and should be dealt with in a therapeutic setting, the effects of more subtle childhood experiences sometimes seem to be neglected.

From my own childhood and family history and the effects past events have on my adult life, I know how much my adult self has been affected by childhood experiences. Through a lot of reading (bibliotherapy), therapy, meditation and research I have come to understand that even more subtle "trauma" can have a significant effect on many aspects of our development, especially when it comes to relationships with others and, more importantly, the relationship with ourselves.

In his book, *Healing the Child Within*, Dr Charles L. Whitfield estimates that only about 5–20 per cent of people grow up with a healthy amount and quality of love, guidance and nurturing. This leaves 80–95 per cent of us not having received enough. I was both surprised and relieved when I read this estimated statistic. On one hand I was surprised and saddened at the extent of "neglect" for want of a better word, and on the other hand it made me feel a little less neurotic and "different".

Daniel Siegel and Mary Hartzell make it clear in *Parenting from the Inside Out* that all of us have leftover issues passed on from generation to generation. When we become parents, it is inevitable that our personal unresolved issues come to the forefront and these issues, if not addressed, will influence our parenting negatively as they can "bias our perceptions, alter our decision-making processes, and create obstacles to collaborate communication with our children". If we don't repair our own historical damage, attachment to our children can suffer greatly as our children "need us to attune to them in order to achieve the physiological balance that enables them to create a coherent mind." This is what Siegel calls the ABC of attachment:

> **A**ttunement: Aligning your own mental state with those of your children. Often accomplished by the contingent sharing of non-verbal signals.

> **B**alance: Your children attain balance of their body, emotions, and states of mind through attunement with you.

> **C**oherence: The sense of integration that is acquired by your children through your relationship with them in which they are able to come to feel both internally integrated and interpersonally connected to others.

My own upbringing was very traditional and from the outside looking in we were a pretty respectable family: my father was a teacher and my mother was a stay-at-home mum taking care of me and my two younger siblings. There was no alcoholism, child sexual abuse, physical abuse or other major trauma during my childhood, and from all appearances we were a "happy" family, especially when we were younger. We lived on the edge of a small village in rural Germany and had our own home with a large garden just beside a beautiful forest. We spent most of our time outdoors, and both my mum and dad put in great effort in raising us as healthily as they could, growing all our own vegetables in the garden and instilling a great awareness for our environment and our responsibility for it. We attended Mass every weekend and were raised in the Catholic faith with prayers at lunch and bedtime.

When we grew a little older I guess the cracks started to show more. My father was quite an overpowering character. Basically he was the patriarch, though I would even call him somewhat of a tyrant at times. Most of my later childhood memories (from about the age of ten) in relation to our family home are tainted by a constant feeling of stress and discomfort. We only ever relaxed when

27

my dad had gone away and we knew he wouldn't be back for hours. I can still hear the sound of the key turning in the door and his stomping footsteps approaching the sitting room door when he would return home, and I physically still tense up as I did as a child. I wasn't really allowed to bring friends home, both as a child and later as a teenager, but I was so ashamed of my father's moody behaviour that I never really wanted to bring anybody to our house anyway.

After a lot of inner work, I realise now that we were quite a dysfunctional family and the roles we adopted as a result were unhealthy for our further development. I involuntarily took on the role of protecting my mother because from a young age I had a very strong sense of justice. My father would criticise literally everything my mum did: questioning her decisions, complaining about lunch, moaning about her buying the wrong bread or ham. This went on incessantly on a daily basis. My mother just stayed mute. The older I became, the angrier I got at my father, and as my mother wouldn't stand up for herself, I felt I had to. I would often stand between them and defend my mother. Now I know that this was not my responsibility, but rather than my mother preventing me from taking on that position, she continued to lean on me well into my adult life. From much too young an age our roles were reversed and to this day I have never really had a mother figure to look to for guidance and support. I remember as a young teenager pleading with my mother to separate from my father; the constant tension and fighting became unbearable. As the tension grew stronger throughout the years, I had to find strategies to protect myself. Internally I built up a safe wall around myself, and only later on in life I started to question my inability to connect to my personal emotions as well as to the people that were supposed to be closest to me i.e. my family, friends, boyfriends etc. I also started to avoid home as much as I could, staying with friends or at the riding stables nearby. Especially in my teenage years I never felt "at home" or deeply rooted within my family or home, and there has been a great sense of loss and longing ever since.

This dysfunctional system had a major effect on me, and as I started the journey of self-discovery I was surprised to find a few truths that I would never have thought possible. Slowly but surely I started to untangle the strands of guilt, shame, anger, self-loathing and hidden emotions, and the realisation that the key to a lot of my emotional issues was to be found in my childhood and the impaired attachment to both of my parents.

I had already written most of this chapter when unexpectedly I had the opportunity to attend Dr Daniel Siegel's conference on developmental trauma entitled: "An Interpersonal Neurobiological Approach to Transforming Developmental Trauma into Integration and Resiliency" in Cork City, Ireland. What had caught my attention in the promotional description was the following sentence: "How early life experiences and relationships interact with the nervous system and the developing mind to shape who we become." I had already been a big fan of Dr Siegel's work and had read many of his books, some of which are quoted in this book. He manages to relate the scientific basis of how our brains function in a very approachable manner that even us non-scientists can understand, and the delivery of this conference was eye-opening and inspiring. His explanation as to how trauma of any kind affects our brain was as follows: when we experience trauma our bodies produce high doses of cortisol (as a response to stress) for an extended period of time. Cortisol is neuro-toxic, which means that it either inhibits the growth of new neurons in our brain, or it actually even destroys already-present synapses and neurons. Imagine a network of roads connecting villages, towns and cities. If these roads were destroyed and even some of the villages were damaged, what would this do to a region? Connections would be interrupted; trade and travel wouldn't be possible. This is the same process in the brain. When synapses (roads) and neurons (villages) are damaged, the exchange between different areas of the brain is disrupted and the brain's integration becomes impaired. The great news Dr Siegel conveyed was that this damage can be repaired at any stage, for example through mindfulness meditation practice. He said, "Where attention goes, neuro-firing flows, neuro connection grows."

The introduction to mindfulness meditation was one of the most powerful tools I was lucky enough to receive during my own journey. I will be forever grateful for this skill because without it I would still be immersed in suffering and confusion. Mindfulness isn't the magic cure for everything, but it certainly is a very valuable life skill to put things into perspective, to stop and feel ourselves, notice the environment around us and see things more clearly as they really are. Mindfulness can act as a bridge, which will help us to reconnect some of the missing links, and as Dr Siegel explained, reconnecting links is literally the process that takes place in our brains.

Even though I still sometimes struggle with my emotional issues related to my childhood, I can also see that in their own way my parents tried their best to raise us well. Through all the struggles, fights and tension I never doubted that they loved us. I am very grateful for all the gifts, the good things, the life skills, interests and valuable lessons I received from both my mum and dad, both through parenting as well as genes. They instilled respect and care for our planet in me and a great interest and love for nature and animals. We all had to play a part in our family and help out with chores to earn a treat, and that taught me to take nothing for granted and be appreciative. There was never a shortage of anything, and we were always encouraged in our interests and hobbies without being flooded by a full schedule. We were involved and took great interest in sourcing and collecting foods from local producers and went foraging for wild treasures in the forest. From a young age we helped out with the cooking and preserving of the natural produce and all of us have a great appreciation of these skills and good food in general. Our garden was like a treasure chest to us children, and to this day a garden is my sanctuary. My mum is a naturally creative person. I inherited her love for art and crafts, and I'm passing this on to my girls now. There are many things that I am eternally grateful for. Both my mother and father have their own emotional struggles and unresolved issues and unfortunately were not able to keep them away from us children. Nonetheless, the effect their parenting style had on all of us children had far-reaching consequences. Thankfully, through a lot of work on both sides, I have a great relationship with my dad today. I cherish his love and concern, not only for myself but especially for my two daughters.

These experiences and their effect on personal development, even though they might sound quite ordinary and not overly dramatic to some, bring to the forefront the importance of raising our children mindfully. It doesn't take major trauma to impact negatively on our children – it can be quite subtle, and our circumstances and emotional disposition will influence our parenting if we are not aware of it. That doesn't mean that we should hide our emotions. Children have a sixth sense and the worst we can do is lie to them rather than telling them when we're sad, angry or frustrated. In order to parent mindfully it is so important to take care of ourselves, to pay attention and recognise when we need to stop, take a break, breathe and identify our emotional state in order to parent wisely and compassionately. To say it in Eleanor Brown's words:

"Self-care is not selfish — You can't serve from an empty vessel."

Even the smallest action, a sentence uttered without thinking, a body movement or a touch, can embed itself into a child's memory and have a major impact, either positive or negative, on their future lives and development. We all have these little nuggets of memories throughout our lives — things and words that we have never forgotten and that have shaped our path in life. If we are aware of these moments and of our own emotional state as we interact with our children and with any child in our environment, we can't go wrong. Children need to experience the full spectrum of emotional experiences — anger, sadness and disappointment as well as happiness, excitement and love — but they need to feel supported; they need to know it's OK to feel all of these emotions and that we all feel them sometimes.

Chapter 3

The parent–child relationship

Children have an incredible ability to know whether their parents are interacting with them in a mindful way or they are just being given automated responses because parents are occupied, distracted or even just tired. My three-year-old daughter regularly pulls me up whenever I just automatically answer her rather than mindfully respond to her questions or needs. Even though I might have given her the desired answer, she will say, "Mama, you're not listening, turn your face around!" The meaning is undeniable: "Look at me when we're talking and pay attention!" These instances make me smile because she teaches me mindfulness every day in so many ways without even knowing it. Young children still mostly operate in the "being mode" rather than the "doing mode". It is just their natural state, and everything they do and say is done with their whole being. As Dr Siegel said during the aforementioned conference:

"Secure attachment comes through parental presence."

Siegel mentions the 4 S's of Attachment as the following:
Children need to be:
Seen (in their subjective experience)
Safe
Soothed
In order to develop **S**ecure attachment, or in other words the internal feeling that everything is going to be okay.

Interpersonal neurobiology researchers and theorists emphasise the importance of secure parent–child relationships, not only in the first three years of a child's life but throughout childhood and into adulthood. We now know that not only is a secure parent–child bond emotionally essential for a child, but it is also required for optimal development of the brain, sense of self and the ability to regulate emotion. To put it into simple words, a parent must establish a secure attachment with their child for that child to develop well at all levels: physical, emotional and psychological. Unfortunately, contemporary living often makes this challenging.

Mindfulness can play a key role in helping parents remain emotionally available to their children either through more formal or informal practices and activities. With children, attunement often takes on a more non-verbal form, and parents should be encouraged to "follow their child's lead" by simply noticing what the child is doing and joining in. This can happen through action and through words. When parents allow themselves to be led by the child's thoughts, interests and impulses, this enables them to mindfully experience their child's inner world, and attunement naturally follows.

Parenting is the most challenging, frightening and overwhelming job in the world. Raising the next generation is an important role. There are great expectations and responsibilities attached to being a parent. If you are anything like me, I often feel the pressure that is put on me by society, but mainly I put it on myself – to be the perfect parent and do everything "right", which obviously is unrealistic. All we can do is our best at any given time. Myla and Jon Kabat-Zinn's book, *Everyday Blessings,* is in my view one of the most valuable resources for parents who are interested in mindfulness and mindful parenting. They describe the challenge of parenting as follows:

> Parenting is one of the most challenging, demanding, and stressful jobs on the planet. It is also one of the most important, for how it is done influences in great measure the heart and soul and consciousness of the next generation, their experience of meaning and connection, their repertoire of life skills, and their deepest feelings about themselves and their possible place in a rapidly changing world. Yet those of us who become parents do so virtually without preparation or training, with little or no guidance or support, and in a world that values producing far more than nurturing, doing far more than being.
>
> The best manuals on parenting can sometimes serve as useful references, giving us new ways of seeing situations, and reassuring us, especially in the early years of parenting, or when we are dealing with special problems, that there are various ways to handle things and that we are not alone.
>
> But what these books often do not address is the inner experience of parenting. What do we do with our own mind, for instance? How do we avoid getting swallowed

up and overwhelmed by our doubts, our insecurities, by the real problems we face in our lives, by the times when we feel inwardly in conflict, and the times when we are in conflict with others, including our children? Nor do they indicate how we might develop greater sensitivity and appreciation for our children's inner experience.

To parent consciously requires that we engage in an inner work on ourselves as well as in the outer work of nurturing and caring for our children. The "how-to" advice that we can draw upon from books to help us with the outer work has to be complemented by an inner authority that we can only cultivate within ourselves through our own experience. Such inner authority only develops when we realise, that in spite of all of the things that happen to us that are outside of our control, through our choices in response to such events and through what we initiate ourselves, we are still, in large measure, "authoring" our own lives. In the process, we find our own ways to be in this world, drawing on what is deepest and best and most creative in us. Realising this, we may come to see the importance for our children and for ourselves of taking responsibility for the ways in which we live our lives and for the consequences of the choices we make.

Inner authority and authenticity can be developed to an extraordinary degree if we do that inner work. Our authenticity and our wisdom grow when we purposely bring awareness to our own experience as it unfolds. Over time, we can learn to see more deeply into who our children are and what they need, and take the initiative in finding appropriate ways to nourish them and further their growth and development. We can also learn to interpret their many different, sometimes puzzling signals and to trust our ability to find a way to respond appropriately. Continual attention, examination, and thoughtfulness are essential even to know what we are facing as parents, much less how we might act effectively to help our children to grow in healthy ways.

Parenting is above all uniquely personal. Ultimately, it has to come from deep inside ourselves. Someone else's way of doing things will never do. We each have to find a way that's our own, learning from all useful sources along the way. We have to learn to trust our own instincts and to nourish and refine them.

The last paragraph especially rings home for me. We often compare ourselves, our children and our situation to others, which can put unrealistic pressure on us and our expectations. Everybody and everybody's situation is different and unique, and this is where mindfulness can make a great difference to our families. If we notice and accept ourselves and our children in the here and now, and apply non-judging, patience and kindness to our actions and thoughts, this will serve as a solid base for a more harmonious and connected family life. If we keep comparing ourselves to others from a materialistic, emotional or circumstantial viewpoint, we will never be content, as it is impossible to mimic someone else's life.

If we are really honest with ourselves and pay attention to the smaller details, we often find that we don't really want someone else's life anyway. What we really want is our magnified illusion of what their life consists of in our minds. For example, we may think the Smiths have a bigger house, more money, go on two holidays a year and all look fit and stylish, when the reality is that Mr Smith is hardly at home, Mrs Smith feels very lonely in the big house and their daughter has an eating disorder caused by depression and anxiety. This of course is a very blunt example, but you get the point. I remember hearing someone say: If you sat around a table with a group of people who were asked to leave all of their troubles in a little pile in front of them and everybody had the option of swapping theirs with somebody else's, most people would grab their own pile and run! I have oftentimes thought of this, especially in difficult times, and I have to agree with it. That doesn't mean we're not allowed to dream big dreams and strive for a better life, but do it for yourself and your own life circumstances rather than in competition with your neighbour. This sets an important example for your children. Trusting and loving relationships within the family unit gives children secure roots in life, and mindful interactions and communication are a good starting point for creating positive relationships and future connections free from the erroneous belief that the grass is always greener on the other side.

One contemporary challenge to the goal of deepening our parent–child relationships is the rising influence of peers from a very early age. The increase of "external parenting" especially of very young children is a significant downside to modern life. I know this topic raises its head a couple of times in this book, as the effects are multiple. When parents go back to work after maternity or parental leave, be it by choice or necessity, many of us do not have the luxury of our partner staying at home or even have close family members that are able to take care of our children while we are at work. Oftentimes children attend childcare services from an early age, and due to their very nature children's lives are influenced greatly by their peers rather than by their parents or other adult role models.

As I write, this year's budget (2016), announced by the Irish government, is being debated on the radio. There was an increase in some aspects concerning childcare costs and a major factor in the debate was that parents and close relations are not valued as "childcare providers"; they are basically discriminated against. I couldn't agree more with that side of the argument. Rather than paying, in many cases, barely qualified workers the minimum wage for taking care of our most precious children, would it not make more sense to allow parents to take time off work in order to take care of their children and make sure they grow up in a secure and nourishing home? I believe families should at least have that choice.

TAKING CARE OF OURSELVES AS PARENTS AND AS INDIVIDUALS

"Every baby can be seen as a little Buddha or Zen Master; your own private mindful teacher."

KABAT-ZINN, 1994

If you have ever been on a flight you might remember the steward or stewardess going through the cabin-safety demonstration before take-off. I recall the first time I heard the part about putting on your own oxygen mask before attending to your children or anybody else. I remember being confused initially; there were no further explanations given as to why this was best practice. It was only after thinking about it for a while did it dawn on me that you're no good to anybody else or yourself if you lose consciousness. It is only by taking proper care of yourself that you are able to help others. It has nothing to do with being selfish, quite the opposite actually. If we want to be mindful and attentive parents, we must first take care of our own well-being, physical as well as mental. Only then are we in a position to be authentic and present. There will always be situations in our lives where this might be difficult, but prioritising our own emotional and physical balance will help us get through challenging times more easily.

As was touched on earlier, being a parent can be a great source of stress. Since becoming a mother I have realised it is equally the most wonderful and the most challenging thing that has ever happened to me. It can be quite confusing at times and even generates a huge amount of guilt. How could I possibly have any negative emotions about being a parent? Even worse, how could I ever feel the slightest bit of resentment towards my child? Does this make me a bad mother or person? I could never in my wildest dreams have imagined the emotional turmoil parenthood could bring into my life. The responsibility, the worries and fears, real and imaginary, the additional work – it can all get overwhelming at times, especially when life and individual family situations cause further stress.

I have always been quite an anxious person from early childhood, and stress has been a buddy of mine for as long as I can remember. Much of the time I would have been worried about things directly related to me: What if I get sick? What if I have an accident? What if I fail my exams? What if people don't like me? One of the things that struck me most when my first little girl was born was the intensity of the instant worries and fears for her well-being. Not only that, initially the focus of worry was completely diverted away from myself, only to return with double force from a completely different angle: What if something happens to me and I won't be able to care for her? Without a doubt, parenthood is the most precious and most beautiful gift I have ever received, but the stress and worry it brings should not be underestimated or ignored. From talking to many other parents, I know that I am not alone in this. That is why it is so important to take good care of ourselves in order to be the best parents we can possibly be for our children but also for ourselves as individuals. The following chapter presents what I believe to be an essential method to achieve this: mindfulness.

Chapter 4

What is mindfulness?

Have you ever driven your car and literally wondered how you got to your destination? Have you ever found yourself with the empty chocolate-bar wrapper in your hands and not been able to remember eating it? Have you ever had to go back five pages in a book because you couldn't remember a single word you had read? Sounds familiar? During my first meditation retreat our teacher asked the group this question: "What is the main reason that you are here this weekend?" and many of us, including myself, shared a variation of the same answer: we felt that time was just slipping through our hands; days rolled into weeks into months into years. It's sometimes like Groundhog Day and we can't believe it's Monday, AGAIN! Too scarce are the moments we stop and hold our faces into the sun, savouring a few precious minutes of warmth and peace, but it's these glimpses that we'll remember for a long time: what it felt like, where we were ...

Parents would benefit from attaining a good foundation of mindfulness practice. A basis could be an initial eight-week programme to establish the knowledge and experience needed for regular personal practice. It can be difficult, especially with young children, to get into the routine of regular practice, and nobody knows better than I that there are days or even weeks when formal practice just doesn't happen. The key is not to beat yourself up about it, accept the present situation and try your best to incorporate little moments of informal practice whenever you think of it. The longer you do it, the easier it gets to grab these few minutes here and there to ground yourself into the present moment.

Before we go any further, let's have a look at some definitions and explanations of mindfulness:

In the "Mindfulness Research Guide" David Black gives the following description of Mindfulness:

> Mindfulness is a quality of human consciousness characterized by an accepting awareness of and enhanced attention to the constant stream of lived experience. Being mindful increases engagement with the present moment and allows for a clearer understanding of how thoughts and emotions can impact our health and quality of life. Mindfulness can be cultivated through meditation practice. Mindfulness meditation practices have been formalized in programs such as Mindfulness-Based Stress Reduction (MBSR), Mindfulness-Based Cognitive Therapy (MBCT), and Mindfulness-Based Relapse Prevention (MBRP) as well as other programs. Although mindfulness is an inherent human capacity that has been examined introspectively for millennia, scientific interest in mindfulness is burgeoning in the fields of medicine, psychology, social work, and business, as well as other areas.

In Jon Kabat-Zinn's words: "Mindfulness means paying attention in a particular way: On purpose, in the present moment, and nonjudgmentally."

The Mindful Schools website states: "Bringing awareness to one's experience – mindfulness can be applied to our senses, thoughts, and emotions by using sustained attention and noticing our experience without over-identifying."

Even though some aspects might be repeated, I also want to include here a short article entitled "What is Mindfulness?" by Matthew Brensilver, who is part of the fantastic Mindful Schools Team, as I really think he gives a great understanding and overview of what mindfulness is:

> As mindfulness gains cultural momentum, there is a risk that its definition becomes more muddled. If we are to practice effectively and teach these practices to our students and

communities, conceptual clarity is important. Of course, no single person or group has the authority to provide the one-and-only definition of 'mindfulness'. This is an open and evolving conversation among practitioners, scientists and scholars. We do not claim to offer the definitive version of mindfulness, but instead share a definition that has been productive in our practice and teaching, and is supported by the scientific research on mindfulness.

Mindfulness can be considered a state, a trait or a practice. We can have a moment of mindfulness (state) but also have a habitual tendency of mindfulness (trait). We can do the intentional formal practice of mindfulness using different postures and activities: seated mindfulness, mindful walking or mindful eating, for example. The formal practice of mindfulness leads to more moments of mindfulness and ultimately improved trait-level mindfulness. Higher trait-level mindfulness means that we're more mindful even when we're not consciously trying to be mindful. This is critically important: we're learning to create a healthy habit of mindfulness.

Below is a diagram that highlights two components of mindfulness: present-time awareness and equanimity.

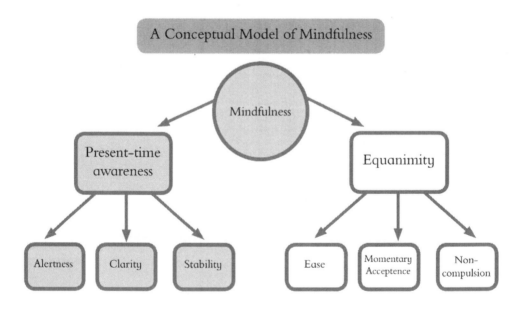

PRESENT–TIME AWARENESS

The first component, present-time awareness, is perhaps more familiar to readers. It refers to a stable, clear and alert awareness of momentary experience. In present-time awareness, we are awake and alive to the moment. We know sensory experience – sights, sounds, sensations, thoughts – and we know that we're knowing. When we're on 'automatic pilot', we are, in fact, knowing something – typically our thoughts – but we don't know that we're knowing. We are all familiar with times when there's virtually no mindfulness present – but we're still having experience. We're still experiencing sights and sounds and sensations and thoughts – but we don't know that's what we're experiencing. Present-time awareness is thus a kind of meta-awareness, where we have rich contact with sensory experience and we know it's sensory experience arising in the field of awareness.

Present-time awareness is depicted as a combination of stability, clarity and alertness. Imagine looking through a telescope at the moon. If the telescope were shaking, it would be difficult to fully take in the sight of the moon. Similarly, stability of our attention is important for present-time awareness. The moon would also be obscured if the lens were out of focus. In mindfulness practice, our 'vision' becomes more clear. We're able to detect more and more subtle features of our experience. Lastly, we must be alert to the present moment. If we looked through a steady and focused telescope but we're really sleepy and lapsing in and out of awareness, we would miss the grandeur of the moon. Mindfulness steadies the attention, focuses the attention, and remains alert to the object of our attention.

EQUANIMITY

While present-time awareness has important benefits on its own, the second component of mindfulness – equanimity, is critically important. Equanimity may be an unfamiliar word, but it has an important meaning in the context of mindfulness practice. Equanimity can be defined as a sense of cognitive-emotional balance where there is no compulsion to act out our preferences. It has a number of connotations: ease, non-reactivity, non-manipulation of experience, and the toleration of the arising, intensification, weakening and disappearance of subjective experiences. Equanimity is the balance point between suppression of experience on the one hand, and entanglement with experience on the other.

Equanimity is often confused with indifference or passive acceptance of suffering in the world. This is a misunderstanding. In the diagram, we include 'momentary acceptance' to denote that equanimity marks our relation to present-time experience – not objective conditions in the world. We can be equanimous with our present-time experience, but be deeply committed to changing and improving the conditions in the world.

In sum, we define mindfulness as attending to present-moment experience with equanimity. Our definition is similar to other common definitions of mindfulness. For example, Jon Kabat-Zinn defined mindfulness as 'the awareness that emerges through paying attention on purpose, in the present moment, and non-judgmentally to the unfolding of experience moment by moment.' In this definition, 'non-judgmentally' relates to the momentary acceptance component of equanimity.

Future research will seek to better understand the components of mindfulness, how they work together, and how they confer benefits in our personal and professional lives. Of course, you can do your own research in the laboratory of your own mind! As you practice, you might examine how present-time awareness and equanimity function in your experience. Perhaps there is another aspect of mindfulness that you feel is important. The exploration will support greater clarity and nuance as we think about, practice, and teach mindfulness.

Mindfulness meditation is rooted in Buddhist tradition: The Pali word for mindfulness meditation *satipatthana* literally translates as "keeping present" (patthana) "awareness" (sati). Mindfulness is the second meditation technique in Buddhist psychology. This technique differs from concentration in the way the attention is directed. Instead of restricting attention to one object, attention is systematically expanded to encompass any physical or mental activity from moment-to-moment with an attitude of detachment and acceptance.

From my own experience I know that there sometimes seems to be a misconception about mindfulness being an intervention that will help people relax, especially when they associate it with the term MBSR (Mindfulness-Based Stress Reduction). Even though it may often be the case that people relax during their meditation practice, this would go against the principles of non-striving and acceptance as we can't "make" ourselves relax. Mindfulness to me is about holding all that arises in awareness – this could be thoughts, physical sensations or emotions of any kind. It's about learning to be with "what is" in a non-reactive way.

I am of the strong belief that mindfulness should ideally be an integral part of every person's life in one form or another. Looking at the main components and foundations of mindfulness it makes sense that each and every one of them should be part of our human existence in order for us to live our lives to the fullest, but also to transform our relationships with ourselves and the people around us. As soppy as it may sound, the world would truly be a better place if we all adopted the key attitudes of mindfulness, which are basically the following important life skills:

- **Non-judging**: Noticing how often we judge our own experience as good (and want to hold on to it), bad (and want to reject it) and neutral (and just want to forget it). In mindfulness we try and be non-judging.

- **Patience**: This is a form of wisdom – really understanding and allowing things to unfold just as they will without pushing or forcing.

- **Kindness**: An attitude of kindness for us and others is an invaluable tool to practise forgiveness and instil love for ourselves and others. This can be particularly helpful in healing difficult relationships, especially our own inner dialogue and often without the knowledge of the other person(s).

- **Trust**: Trusting our judgement, rather than looking outside of ourselves for all the answers, can help to develop confidence in our inner wisdom.

- **Non-striving**: Meditation and mindfulness are unique in not trying to achieve anything. Striving gets in the way with what's going on right now – it is going on anyway, so you may as well be there for it.

- **Beginner's mind**: With a beginner's mind we can see each experience as it really is without preconceived ideas of how we think things should be. We can see things with fresh eyes.

- **Curiosity**: Curiosity helps us to stay with our experience moment by moment. What does it feel like to be anxious? Which part of my body is tense or in pain? What kind of thoughts are passing through?

- **Letting go**: Holding on creates tension and suffering. Letting go and allowing things to move on can create a feeling of freedom and peacefulness.

- **Acceptance**: Accepting ourselves and our situation just as it is right now is the best way to allow change to happen. It clears the path for change.

ALIDINA, 2010; SUTTON, 2012

THE NEUROBIOLOGY OF MINDFULNESS

The first time I was introduced to the neurobiological aspect of mindfulness was when I was a participant in the "Mindful Schools Curriculum Training" some years ago. Chris McKenna, one of the programme directors, gave a comprehensive talk about mindfulness and the brain, which gave a very clear understanding on the effects of mindfulness on our brain mainly based on the work of Dr Daniel Siegel, whom I will be quoting frequently throughout this book, as he has done extensive research in the area of "interpersonal neurobiology". Before listening to Chris I was already convinced about the benefits and positive effects of mindfulness through my own experience and practice, as well as different action research studies I had read. The scientific proof and explanation of mindfulness and the neurobiological processes are absolutely captivating and in my opinion very important to underpin the validity of the benefits and importance of mindfulness, especially when explaining it to parents in a school setting. As this area is very scientific and not my professional background, but crucial all the same, I just want to give a short and simplified version for the purpose of basic understanding:

MINDSIGHT

In his 2010 book, *Mindsight,* Dr Siegel gives a fascinating account of the workings of our brains and in particular the concept of neuroplasticity. Siegel coined the term "mindsight", the meaning of which is, in my view, inherently interconnected with the topic of mindfulness because it describes a focused attention that "allows us to see the internal workings of our own minds." I would even go so far as to say that mindsight is basically the scientific backup for mindfulness. This is invaluable, especially in the area of early intervention with children, as it proves the profound benefits and downright necessity of the introduction of mindfulness-based approaches from an early age. Mindsight helps us to pay attention and be aware of our mental occurrences while staying present. It helps us to pause and stop, and interrupt automated behaviours and responses, thus enabling us to identify thoughts, feelings and emotions. Siegel emphasises the way we label our emotions when identified. He claims there is a significant difference between "I am sad", which is a very limiting self-definition, and "I feel sad", which acknowledges the emotion without being trapped in it. The skills involved in mindsight make it possible to identify the processes and emotions, accepting them, letting them go and with that transforming them. I want to include the following passage from Daniel Siegel's book as it beautifully explains mindsight in a nutshell:

> You can also think of mindsight as a very special lens that gives us the capacity to perceive the mind with greater clarity than ever before. This lens is something that virtually everyone can develop, and once we have it we can dive deeply into the mental sea inside, exploring our own inner lives and those of others. A uniquely human ability, mindsight allows us to examine closely, in detail and in depth, the processes by which we think, feel, and behave. And it allows us to reshape and redirect our inner experiences so that we have more freedom of choice in our everyday actions, more power to create the future, to become the author of our own story. Another way to put it is that mindsight is the basic skill that underlies everything we mean when we speak of having social and emotional intelligence.

NEUROPLASTICITY

The number of synaptic connections i.e. the number of on/off switches for different states of activations in their brains has been calculated as "ten times ten one million times" which is supposed to be more than the number of atoms in our universe. This staggering complexity also means infinite opportunities for our brains to use these "firing patterns", and in Daniel Siegel's opinion we are limiting ourselves if we get stuck in certain patterns. As little as thirty years ago, many scientists still believed the brain was fully formed at a young age. Now we know that the brain keeps developing and growing until the age of twenty-five, and after that it continues to produce as many as 10,000 new neurons every day – right up until the day we die. One of the most profound findings of modern neuroscience is that something as simple as training our attention on one thing, and bringing it back to that one thing over and over again, as it is done in mindfulness meditation for example, has the power to shape our brain's firing patterns. It may actually change the structure and size of certain areas of the brain, especially those areas that are responsible for managing emotions like anger, sadness, frustration and fear. This means we can actually increase the size of the areas of the brain that control stressful emotions and decrease the size of the areas that generate them. Humans have the unique ability to reshape and redirect the neural pathways in our brains, which brings us to the concept of neuroplasticity.

I will try and give you a simplified version of the description Siegel gives of the development of our brains: when we are born our brains are immature with the neurons lacking extensive connections to one another. This gives us an openness to experience, which is crucial for learning. Even though I have no professional knowledge of neuroscience I have always been in awe of the unbelievable capacity for learning especially in the first few years of a child's life. A neuro-typical child will learn to walk, use their body in meaningful ways, talk, make social connections and learn about their environment in the first four to five years of their lives. Siegel puts this into a scientific context, explaining that a "massive proliferation of synapses" occurs during the first years of life, which are dependent on genes, chance and experiences. Some areas of our personalities are less open to the influence of experience than others: our temperaments, for example, seem to be more predetermined by genes and chance and are present before we're even born. I found this particularly interesting because I had always been fascinated by the "ready-made" personalities of very young children who display different personality traits despite sharing the same gene pool and upbringing.

From the very beginning of our lives, our brain is directly shaped by interactions. The experiences we have in our relationships and interactions with our environment stimulate "neural firing" and basically build and shape our brain. Our personality as we grow up is put together like an intricate jigsaw made up of genes, chance and experiences all influencing our preferences, habits and behaviours. Thankfully nothing is "written in stone" as, according to Siegel, focusing our attention in specific therapeutic ways can help to override and divert old patterns into new healthier responses. In his book he explains the intricate neurobiological processes involved, which I won't go into. In layman's terms we as humans have the capacity to "voluntarily change a firing pattern that was laid down involuntarily". Our brain can find new pathways, previously separated areas can become integrated and the brain as a whole can become more interconnected. This results in the mind becoming more flexible and adaptive. The Principles of Neuroplasticity according to Siegel are:

- Relationships

- Sleep

- Nutrition

- Aerobic Exercise

- Humour

- Novelty

- Close paying of attention

In an interview with James Porter, the founder and president of StressStop.com, Daniel Siegel explains that thanks to breakthroughs in brain-imaging technology we can now physically see the changes in the brains of mindfulness meditators. The results of different brain scans reveal that experienced mindfulness meditators can increase the size of the mid-prefrontal cortex, the area of the brain directly responsible for controlling our reaction to stress, and decrease the size of the amygdala, the area of the brain that responds to or creates stress. These findings are crucial in providing proof of the capacity of our brain to re-structure itself physically when "exercised" through mindfulness.

A SHORT SUMMARY OF THE TERM "INTEGRATION OF THE BRAIN"

Our brains are the most complex structure you could imagine. My mum did a course in kinesiology especially geared towards learning when we were in primary school, and I remember her "making us do" different exercises every morning. She explained that we had a right and a left side of the brain which had different functions: the right side was more responsible for our creative skills; the left side was the more logical, calculating part of the brain. With these exercises, she explained, we would help the two sides work together better, helping us to concentrate and learn more easily and efficiently. We probably just rolled our eyes but went along with another one of her "fads". Many years later, when I was a teacher myself, I found myself on a course for professional development about exactly this very topic. Mum was certainly ahead of the times in these things. The scientific reality of how our brains work is a little bit more complicated than just separating a left and a right hand side, as our brain has many different areas with different responsibilities. As Daniel Siegel and Tina Payne Bryson put it in their book, *The Whole-Brain Child*: "It's almost as if our brain has multiple personalities – some rational, some irrational; some reflective, some reactive. No wonder we can seem like different people at different times!"

For our mental health and overall well-being it is important that all parts of our brain work well together. This "working well together" is called "integration". Integration is what makes all the different parts of our brain work "as one". On his website (www.drdansiegel.com) Siegel gives the following explanation of integration:

> For the brain, integration means that separated areas with their unique functions, in the skull and throughout the body, become linked to each other through synaptic connections. These integrated linkages enable more intricate functions to emerge—such as insight, empathy, intuition, and morality.

A result of integration is kindness, resilience, and health. Terms for these three forms of integration are a coherent mind, empathic relationships, and an integrated brain.

Siegel also explained that for the brain to be integrated it takes two "interactive processes" to occur, one being differentiation, the other linking the differentiated areas. He illustrated the concept of integration beautifully with the example of a choir at the conference I attended recently. Dan Siegel asked for some volunteers among the conference participants to form a choir. First of all he sang a note which the choir picked up and held for a few seconds. There was linkage as the choir members all sang together, but no differentiation as everybody just held the same note. The second part of the demonstration involved all participants blocking their ears and "belting out" any song that came to mind as loud as they could, which was a little challenging on the ear to say the least. In this example there was very clear differentiation but no linkage whatsoever. Lastly he asked all choir members to agree on a song they were all going to sing together. They chose a rendition of "Danny Boy" and the result was quite amazing, displaying clearly that differentiation (harmonies, different voices i.e. soprano, baritone, alto etc.) and linkage led to integration, facilitating perfect self-organisation.

As mentioned above, mindfulness meditation and activities have proven to promote the integration of the brain. Through mindfulness exercises new neurons and linkages are grown and existing connections are improved. The integration of the brain has multiple knock-on benefits on our own well-being and our relationships, and it is one of the reasons why mindfulness is such an important skill to learn and teach to our children.

Daniel Siegel has developed the "Wheel of Awareness", an exercise to promote integration of the brain. This exercise is basically a form of mindfulness meditation as it moves and focuses our attention to our senses, our physical sensations, our mental experiences such as thoughts and memories and finally our connections to the external world such as other people, our environment and our planet in general. Regular practice "can liberate the mind from ingrained patterns of cognition and emotion and help you emerge with a more expansive sense of awareness". You can download the exercise for free from Daniel

Siegel's website (www.drdansiegel.com) and include it in your daily routine as a regular mindfulness exercise. I have included an adaption for children in the practical part, which consists of an actual wheel for them to use as a visual aid.

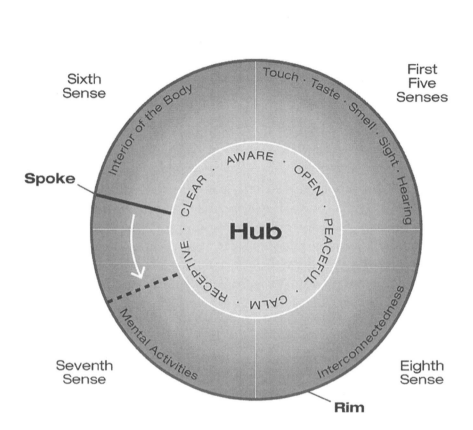

Chapter 5

Why introduce mindfulness to children?

The introduction of mindfulness to children might be more important today than ever. Naturally, childhood nowadays is very different from how I remember growing up. I don't necessarily want to say one is good and one is bad, but I do strongly feel that children today grow up with too many distractions, schedules, technology and general "busyness".

I grew up in rural Germany, and even though my parents supported our interests such as music, sports and art, most of our free time was spent outside, playing in the streets and forest with friends, or at home with Mum in the house or in the garden. There were no "play dates" and constant adult supervision, but plenty of fresh air, wet clothes, scratches and bruises from building tree houses in all weathers or riding our bikes and scooters. Television time consisted of *Sesame Street* after dinner, just before we went to bed, and I never felt deprived. We all slept well even though bedtime was at seven o'clock because we were happily exhausted from physical activity and lots of adventures. We all had a close connection to nature, the elements and the seasons. All of our vegetables were grown in our own garden and were supplemented by foraging seasonal wild delicacies such as blueberries, raspberries, blackberries, chanterelle and cep mushrooms. To this day I know exactly how it smelt when it was about to snow and how the water from the forest spring tasted.

Family life was very important, especially in our younger years. Mum was a full-time homemaker, and we spent a lot of time together making things, playing, going for walks, singing and dancing, but we also had the daily responsibility of doing simple chores in and around the house. Mealtimes were spent as a family at the dinner table where the day and everybody's "experiences" could be reviewed. Don't get me wrong, as I wrote in an earlier chapter, we encountered many of the same problems families face nowadays, and things certainly weren't always as rosy as it might sound. Like any other person we carry some baggage with us, but at least we weren't subjected to an overwhelming amount of social stress, technology and media, and our connection to nature and our environment gave us strong roots to grow from.

It saddens me to see how deprived many children are nowadays of such simple yet precious and important experiences, and how their young lives already are the source of stress. Nowadays, many parents are either forced to or choose to both work full-time. From a young age children are often raised by people outside the family unit for the majority of their day. In addition, most children seem to have a very busy schedule even outside of school. I most certainly agree that children should be supported in their interests and talents, but a full weekly schedule often puts them under pressure. There is little time left over for fun and enjoyment, for some "free time" to just be a child. Paradoxically, even though children's lives seem to be highly scheduled, it appears that children grow up with fewer rules. From my professional experience as a teacher, I notice children and teenagers having less and less respect for others and, importantly,

for themselves. There seems to be an increase in bullying, body-image issues, a lack of concentration, challenging behaviours and other issues that make both teaching and learning more and more difficult.

The majority of early childhood, especially child's play, should be experienced more in the "being mode" rather than the "doing mode". Children are completely immersed in the moment and in their play, completely present in the moment. Sometimes, if we're lucky, we can get a little glimpse of that precious feeling when we really let ourselves be present in play with our children or the children we teach or care for.

Of course we live in different times and it would be naïve of me to think that we can turn back the clock; we all have to accept and move with societal changes, but we also need to ensure that we don't let the price of changing times be paid for by our children. We need to implement coping strategies and programmes to make sure children have a chance to still grow up into confident, happy, kind, loving and creative adults, despite the challenges they face. Mindfulness can play a substantial role in arming our children with such strategies.

Susan Kaiser Greenland even goes so far as stating that mindfulness is the new ABC for children: Attention, Balance, Compassion. She writes, "By practising mindfulness, kids learn life skills that help them soothe and calm themselves, bring awareness to their inner and outer experience, and bring a reflective quality to their actions and relationships."

In *Sitting Still Like a Frog,* Eline Snel sums it up as follows:

> Kids are curious and inquisitive by nature. They are keen to learn things, tend to live in the moment, and can be extremely attentive. But like adults, kids are often too busy. They are tired, easily distracted, and restless. Many children do too much and have too little time to just 'be'. They grow up fast. Sometimes they have to juggle a dozen balls at once socially and emotionally, at home and in school. Add to this all the things they have to learn and memorise, and it soon becomes too much.

ADOLESCENCE: PRUNING AND MYELINATION

From a scientific point of view, there is actually an even more critical component at play to support the importance of mindfulness exercises from a young age. In his book *Brainstorm,* Daniel Siegel provides an eye-opening explanation about what happens to children's brains once they enter into adolescence. During the childhood years our brains "overproduce" neurons and synapses, and when we enter the "pubertal" period (at about eleven years of age in girls and twelve and a half in boys) a process called "pruning" takes place. Pruning literally means the pruning away of excess neurons and synapses that aren't used anymore; only the connections we've been using are retained. As Siegel puts it, "Attention streams energy and information through specific circuits and activates them. The more you use a circuit, the stronger it gets. The less you use a circuit, the more likely it may get pruned away during adolescence. How you focus your attention throughout life and especially during the adolescent period plays an important role in shaping the growth of the brain." This explains why it is so important to foster and support certain skills in childhood before adolescence begins, as our brains are shaped by how we focus our attention.

The second process Siegel describes, that takes place during the same time, is called "myelination": a "sheath of myelin" is laid down over the membranes among the remaining interlinked neurons enabling a faster and more effective flow of information. During adolescence our knowledge and skills become more focused and specific, and due to the focused attention on these circuits, we grow new neurons and linkages. The laying down of myelin makes these circuits faster, more coordinated and effective, which as a result enables us to make wiser decisions, use our intuition and see "the bigger picture", which Siegel calls "gist thinking".

The adolescent period can also unveil potential mental health problems such as depression and bi-polar disorder, which is where the importance of mindfulness comes in. Some children have a predetermined vulnerability towards some conditions, and after pruning takes place these conditions can be unmasked due to the insufficient number of neurons. According to Siegel, these vulnerabilities can have varying causes including genes, toxic exposure and traumatic childhood experiences. Another contributing factor that might intensify the pruning process is additional stress, which increases the potential of activating mental health conditions at this age. It is of vital importance to seek help as soon as possible if a child/adolescent presents with mental health issues. Early diagnosis and intervention can make a big difference and reduce stress which in turn will reduce excessive pruning. As Dr Siegel explained in a recent conference, the early introduction of mindfulness training before entering adolescence could help to repair vulnerabilities and increase the number of neurons and synapses to an extent that even after pruning there would be enough connections remaining to prevent various mental health conditions developing with the onset of adolescence. Even though I am an advocate for mindfulness meditation and have both practised and studied it for many years, I was blown away by these significant findings. If nothing else convinces people about the validity and importance of a mindful approach, this certainly should.

HELPING CHILDREN TO IDENTIFY THEIR EMOTIONS AND FEELINGS

Identifying and reading our own and other's emotions is a crucial part of social communication. It is also a significant part of our own emotional development. As emotions are quite an abstract concept, young children especially find it difficult to decode their feelings and emotions, which can often lead to confusion, frustration and challenging behaviours. Even for us adults it can sometimes be difficult to identify precisely how we feel, as every emotion has different intensities and occurrences.

THE "ATLAS OF EMOTIONS"

The Dalai Lama commissioned Dr Paul Ekman, a pioneer in the study of emotions, and his daughter Dr Eve Ekman to develop the "Atlas of Emotions" (www.atlasofemotions.org), a fantastic resource for promoting emotional well-being in all of us. The website is based on Ekman's study, "What scientists who study emotions agree about", for which he sent out a survey to 248 scientists in the field. Although the Ekmans believe there is strong evidence for more than a dozen emotions, they focused the Atlas they created on just the five emotions that more than 70% of the scientists who study emotion believe there is compelling evidence for: Anger, Fear, Disgust, Sadness and Enjoyment. Consensus was reached that these were the universal emotions all humans have in common, regardless of where or how they grew up. Emotions by their very nature are fluid and greatly vary in intensity and frequency, which is beautifully illustrated in the Atlas of Emotions.

These are the descriptions given of the five universal emotions:

Anger – We get angry when something blocks us or when we think we're being treated unfairly.
Fear – Our fear of danger lets us anticipate threats to our safety.
Disgust – Feeling disgusted by what is toxic helps us to avoid being poisoned, physically or socially.
Sadness – Sadness is a response to loss, and feeling sad allows us to take timeout and show others that we need support.
Enjoyment – Enjoyment describes the many good feelings that arise from experiences both novel and familiar.

The Atlas also gives the following associated aspects of each emotion:

States – States of an emotion can be felt mildly, extremely, or somewhere in-between. For example, the states of

58

enjoyment from mild to extreme: sensory pleasure, rejoicing, compassion/joy, amusement, Schadenfreude, relief, peace, pride, wonder, excitement and ecstasy.

Actions – We respond to emotional states with our actions.

Triggers – A trigger is something around us or in our own minds that causes us to feel an emotion.

Moods – Moods are longer lasting cousins of an emotion that cause us to feel the related emotion repeatedly without any clear trigger.

Experiencing Calm – A calm, balanced frame of mind helps us understand our changing emotions. We can reach calmness through developing an awareness of our emotions: what triggers them, how we experience them and how we can respond constructively.

As you can see, even though there are "only" five basic emotions, these can be felt and acted upon in a multitude of ways, which can be difficult for us adults to differentiate. You can only imagine how confusing and frustrating this must be for developing children and teenagers, especially when confronted with a stressful situation.

EMOTION REGULATION

Our family had to deal with some very difficult and stressful situations, so I enrolled in a fantastic course on dealing with difficult emotions a couple of years ago. It was facilitated by Matthew Brensilver and the fantastic Mindful Schools Team. This course was a lifesaver, as it gave clear insight into what actually happens when we are experiencing difficult emotions. In order to understand why mindfulness can support us in dealing with difficult emotions in particular, it is important to know the stages of an emotional response. Based on the study "Process Model of Emotion Regulation" by Gross & Thompson, there are four stages or "elements of an emotional encounter". First of all, there is a **situation** triggering the emotion and its impact depends strongly on the **attention** to certain aspects of the situation. Next there is the assessment or the **appraisal** of the situation, meaning we try and make sense of what is happening. Finally there is our response or **reaction** to the situation.

According to Gross & Thompson there are different strategies (emotion regulation) with which we can influence, change or avoid situations triggering a negative emotion or navigate a stressful episode. Firstly, there is **situation modification**, when we intervene during the situation and modify it: I am very allergic to perfume and certain flowers, and if I sit too close to a person wearing perfume in a coffee shop, I have to get up and move away because as well as a possible allergic reaction I can also get very anxious. Secondly, there is **situation selection** where we pre-empt a stressful, annoying or worrying situation: I normally avoid restaurants and cafes that regularly have large flower displays. According to their research, this effective strategy is often employed subconsciously. Unfortunately it is not always possible to avoid certain situations. The third mode of emotion regulation is **attention deployment**, and the practice of mindfulness exercises could be seen as a form of this. While in stressful situations, we tend to focus on our thoughts and go into heightened problem-solving mode, often developing into repetitive (ruminating) patterns; this only adds to our stress levels. In mindfulness we learn to direct our attention away from the thought explosion towards the overall experience by focusing on physical sensations and our breath. Becoming aware of the bodily manifestations of differing emotions can be hugely beneficial in order to come through an emotionally challenging situation. The fourth example of emotion regulation is **cognitive reappraisal**, which is seeing a situation from a different angle to help us to modulate our emotional reaction to a situation. Last but not least, Gross & Thompson mention the mode of **response modulation,** which is useful once the emotion has arisen and we want to find a constructive strategy of dealing with it. This could involve finding a quiet place away from people and shouting out our anger or frustration, or we could look for support from friends and family. It could also take the form of a mindfulness exercise such as a short breathing break or body scan. One of my biggest fears is the fear of flying. I like to travel so I have to manage this fear, especially because I don't want to "pass it on" to my children. One of the most helpful sentences for me in these situations is: "What is happening right now?" I direct my awareness to my breathing, to my feet touching the ground, to the sounds I hear, my environment around me and to the sensations in my body. Occasionally, if it's possible, I sneak away to the restroom to get some quiet time, as the "busyness" of an airport seems to accelerate my anxiety. Mindfulness has helped me to manage my fear effectively; even though I still don't love flying, it supports me greatly in "getting on with it".

STRESS

Thousands of years ago "stress" was basically our survival instinct, and it served us very effectively. We are hardwired for survival, and the "hot" emotions such as surprise and disgust tell us instantly: "Beware! There's something not quite right", "There's a predator approaching" or "It's safer not to eat this!" The "fight or flight" response might be the best-known example of our survival instinct and is triggered by a situation that could potentially threaten our existence. The "fight or flight" response works on three different levels: emotionally we might feel intense fear or anger; psychologically our senses are heightened, enabling a quick response; and physically, adrenaline rushes through our body, our heart rate increases and the blood flow is directed to areas where it might be most needed, thus increasing strength and stamina. The problem is that human lives were very basic and threatening situations were obvious, foreseeable and understandable. Modern human life has become much more complex and the "fight or flight" response not only is triggered much more often due to this complexity, but it can also prevent us from handling a situation appropriately as neither fighting nor fleeing solves most modern-day situations. Jim Taylor, a professor of psychology at the University of San Francisco, even goes so far as asking: "Is our survival instinct failing us?" It is certainly a paradox if one of our greatest contemporary challenges is to control our most basic reactions in order to survive.

I recently saw a short report about children and stress on a German television channel (KiKa), where I learned that psychological stress, as we know it, is actually a very new concept. It was first identified by the American scientist Hans Selye in 1936 but was largely rejected by the scientific community until much later. The psychologist Dr John Mason subsequently spent many years measuring stress hormone levels in people subjected to various conditions and situations; this was possible thanks to new technologies available in the 1960s. It was apparently not until the 1970s when the "stress concept" was first recognised in medical circles, and it was as recent as the 1990s before it was widely used as a term. Even though this was news to me, I wasn't really surprised because it aligns with my view of the effects of a changing society and modern lifestyle. As Eline Snel said, children often have to "juggle too many balls" causing them to be stressed, and according to the above-mentioned report as many as 30 per cent of children nowadays suffer from stress. Many would argue that the figures are much higher. But what exactly is stress?

WHAT IS STRESS?

The Oxford Dictionary gives the following definition of psychological stress: "A state of mental or emotional strain or tension resulting from adverse or demanding circumstances."

A medical definition of stress according to www.medicinenet.com is:

> In a medical or biological context stress is a physical, mental, or emotional factor that causes bodily or mental tension. Stresses can be external (from the environment, psychological, or social situations) or internal (illness, or from a medical procedure). Stress can initiate the "fight or flight" response, a complex reaction of neurologic and endocrinologic systems.

According to Sonia J. Lupien, the scientific director of the Centre for Studies on Human Stress (CSHS) in Montreal, Canada, all stressors have something in common. Scientific research has identified that for a situation to be stressful it must contain one of the, pardon the pun, N.U.T.S. characteristics:

N: **Novelty** – something new and unknown.
U: **Unpredictability** – you didn't see it coming.
T: **Threat of the ego** – a feeling of threat to your competence and/or character.
S: **Sense of control** – Feeling you are losing control of a situation.

In relation to childhood stress, I would like to add one factor to the N.U.T.S. concept and that is simply "too much, too fast, too soon". I don't have any scientific research to back this suggestion up; it's just my personal opinion, derived from my experience. Simply put, children nowadays are bombarded with too much at too young an age. They are often developmentally not in a position to put into perspective and cope with all the demands, the information, the busyness, the challenges and resulting worries. Children are not given the opportunity enough to just be children. Let me put it into a more extreme and maybe initially confusing statement: Children are not given the opportunity to get bored. Are you raising your eyebrows? If so, I can completely understand this reaction. But think about it. Why are we so obsessed with making sure our children are constantly being entertained, educated, trained, babysat, taught and mothered every minute of every day until they go to bed? There seems to be little time for children just to find some stillness and quiet. Not only can this constant "being on the go" be a source of stress, there are also too few opportunities for children to get bored in order to spark their imagination and creativity. I believe that some of the greatest inventions might have been created out of boredom. Serving everything to children on a plate, as well-meant as it is, actually stifles children's initiative, independence and imagination. I myself was reminded of this only a couple of days ago when one of my daughters called me over and complained: "Mummy, you're not entertaining us!"

When children feel stressed it has a detrimental effect on all areas of their lives. Stress is a very abstract concept to understand. Children might say they are unhappy, listless or tired, but they are actually, in reality, often too overwhelmed and confused to identify and untangle the emotions, thoughts and feelings that affect them. Teaching children skills to observe and identify their feelings, emotions and thoughts non-judgementally is essential for them to make sense of what is happening to them and alleviate a lot of confusion. It will also help them (and us) to see a situation for what it is and find constructive solutions.

Another important factor after identification and observation is being able to talk about emotional issues. Oftentimes one of the most difficult aspects of stress is the feeling of being alone, the fear of talking about something we can't even put into words properly. The earlier we teach these skills to our children – and very importantly internalise them ourselves – the more it will become a natural part of their/our lives and interactions. Children will also realise they are not alone with these problems and feelings, and that in itself is a very powerful support. I want to specifically look a little closer into one of the most detrimental results of emotional/psychological stress: worry.

63

The conundrum of worry

"Worry does not empty tomorrow of its sorrow, it empties today of its strength."

LEO BUSCAGLIA

"I am an old man and have known a great many troubles, but most of them never happened."

MARK TWAIN

"Worry is imagination used poorly."

CHRISTINE HASSLER

"If a problem is fixable, if a situation is such that you can do something about it, then there is no need to worry. If it's not fixable, then there is no help in worrying. There is no benefit in worrying whatsoever."

HIS HOLINESS THE DALAI LAMA XIV

I know first-hand the negative effects of worry. I am, by my own admission, a worrier, and I have had to put a great amount of work and effort into managing my worries; my success varies. My husband rightly tells me that I often jump straight to the worst possible outcome of a situation. Mark Twain's quote above, about experiencing many troubles in my life, most of which have never happened, makes me smile knowingly. Some years ago, my best friend and I were chatting and she mused about how similar we were. I looked at her in disbelief, laughed and said, "If the two of us were any less similar we would probably be enemies." She is my hero in her attitude to life, and even though I am sure she worries sometimes, as we all do, she never seems to worry unnecessarily. Some years ago she voluntarily applied for a job in Kabul, Afghanistan and currently lives in Palestine with her partner and two young children. Her work sometimes includes trips into the Gaza Strip! Everyone experiences worry at some stage in their lives; it's a natural emotion and shows that we care. However, not everyone experiences it the same way and to the same degree.

The problem is when worry becomes a default reaction. When every little thought and scenario takes on a life of its own, spinning a web of multiple imaginary disastrous outcomes, our minds can take off on autopilot and soon, without us even noticing, our heads and hearts are spinning. One of the most detrimental phrases is the famous "What if…?" In this scenario, worry will have multiple negative effects on all areas of our lives including low self-esteem, limited confidence, a constant feeling of dread, reduced enjoyment of life, anxiety and limited concentration, to name but a few. For children, inflated worry will have an effect on their overall development. It will influence their social connections, their learning, their confidence, their enjoyment of being a child and all the areas this will have a ripple effect on. One of the most important remedies to counteract worrying, in my opinion and experience, is the practice of mindfulness. If we catch our thoughts racing off on autopilot and bring ourselves back into the present moment, we can give ourselves a breather and observe what is really happening. For children, the skill of mindfulness is essential in order to bring about thought patterns that will counteract the automated responses of their often worried minds and guide them towards a different, healthier direction. The earlier children learn these tools the more they will be able to find strategies to cope with stressful situations.

A mindful parenting and teaching approach can be an opportunity to create trusting relationships where emotional stress and issues can be identified and talked about. Solutions and supports can be found, and this will hopefully have an all-around positive effect on our home and beyond.

Chapter 6

We need more kindness in this world

"Kindness is the language which the deaf can hear and the blind can see."

MARK TWAIN

Long before I became interested in the actual practice of mindfulness meditation I had been fascinated by people like Mahatma Ghandi, Nelson Mandela, the Dalai Lama, Thich Nhat Hanh and other people that had chosen a peaceful and kind way of life even in the midst of desperate life situations. When Nelson Mandela was released I read a few articles about him, and it baffled me how somebody could be so free of bitterness and resentment after decades of wrongful imprisonment. His famous quote, "As I walked out the door toward the gate that would lead to my freedom, I knew if I didn't leave my bitterness and hatred behind, I'd still be in prison," has had a profound impact on me and I often think about it. There is no truer statement.

One of the key attitudes in mindfulness is kindness: kindness towards others, ourselves and the world we live in. If every person had kindness as their number one priority when interacting, the world would certainly be a better place. Not only that, psychologists, such as Martin Seligman, have proven that doing an act of kindness "produces the single most reliable momentary increase in well-being of any exercise" that has been tested. In other words, both showing and receiving kindness makes us happy and increases our well-being.

Children today grow up witnessing too much negativity and carelessness, much of which is filtering down from the leaders at the very top (I am writing this in the aftermath of the US Presidential

Election 2016). Leaders should be role models and demonstrate moral and humane behaviour that will filter down through society to our children and our peers. The modern media outlets make it so much harder for us parents and educators to protect young children from negative and worrying news, and children have to cope with the fallout. In this situation, it is more important than ever that children are taught about kindness, that even though they might hear or see otherwise in the media or in their own schoolyard, they need to learn that it is important to treat other beings kindly, that every person has a right to be treated with respect and care.

Amongst others this is one of the reasons why an awareness and identification of their own emotions and feelings is so important for children. Once children realise the effect people's actions and words, good or bad, have on their own emotions and well-being, they will be able to practice what is often called "theory of mind". In other words, they will be able to put themselves into someone else's shoes. In order for children to understand kindness, they must know what it means to be unkind also, or what it feels like when we are treated in an unkind way. The best way to teach children about emotional issues is to use concrete examples from their own experience pool as well as story-based examples, as this area can be very abstract for children. Brainstorming, for example, can be a good starting point.

Children need to experience kindness in words and actions to learn how to trust, love and be compassionate to others. I know myself that it can be difficult to always have an attitude of kindness, especially in challenging situations when we're treated unfairly or even downright badly. Everybody will have phases when they will feel angry, disappointed, hurt and even want revenge or justice, and it's okay to have these feelings as long as we don't react to them without pausing and evaluating the situation first. When we really examine our natural feelings of anger, dislike and even hate, we will notice very quickly that the only person we are harming with these emotions is ourselves. If we really pay attention and even think back to certain scenarios, we might remember the angry dialogues in our head repeating and repeating (ruminating) like a broken record making us more and more unhappy and upset. We often don't even have the "real" confrontation in order to clear the air or rectify misunderstandings. One specific formal mindfulness exercise that can help break or at least ease the cycle of these unhelpful emotions is "loving-kindness meditation", which is basically a training to tone our kindness muscles. Like our muscles, our brain can be trained by exercising certain areas, and as explained in the section about neuroplasticity, new pathways can be formed for healthier attitudes and coping strategies. For children we can include many small activities and reminders in our daily routines, and children love being involved in "small acts of kindness". I have included some ideas for kindness activities in the practical part.

The most important aspect of encouraging our children to be kind is providing a good example. Children learn many things by imitation, especially mirroring their most important role models: their parents and teachers. We need to always be aware of our own words and actions, most importantly when our children are present, and try to show kindness in our daily interactions wherever we can. Kindness is love, and when children feel loved, they are able to connect with others and more importantly themselves in positive and nurturing ways. However, kindness does not mean that we have to accept hurtful or unfair behaviour of others, quite the contrary. But when children feel loved and supported their confidence grows and they will be able to stand their ground without having to lash out or getting into frustrating confrontations.

I know myself that sometimes we ask ourselves the questions: how can I make a difference in this world? How can a small act of kindness make a difference when there are so many people on this Earth, so many problems, so much poverty, so much injustice and hatred? Is there really any point making the effort? I often get overwhelmed by a feeling of helplessness, frustration and even anger. This is when I remember the following story, which is based on Loren Eiseley's story "The Star Thrower". It is a beautiful illustration as to how every small act of kindness can make a big difference to somebody:

THE STAR THROWER

A man was walking on the beach one day and noticed a boy who reached down, picked up a starfish and threw it in the ocean. As he approached, he called out, 'Hello! What are you doing?'

The boy looked up and said, 'I'm throwing starfish into the ocean.'

'Why are you throwing starfish into the ocean?' asked the man.

'The tide stranded them. If I don't throw them in the water before the sun comes up, they'll die,' came the answer.

'Surely you realise that there are miles of beach, and thousands of starfish. You'll never throw them all back, there are too many. You can't possibly make a difference.'

The boy listened politely, then picked up another starfish. As he threw it back into the sea, he said, 'It made a difference to this one.'

In the original story, the narrator is then inspired by the "Star Thrower" to join him and pick up and throw starfish back into the ocean himself, which is exactly what any act of kindness does – it inspires and encourages others to do the same. I recently saw a beautifully produced clip on Facebook about an act of kindness that was paid forward many years later and ended with the recipient reading a note which said:

"A single act of kindness creates an endless ripple."

Let's all be "Star Throwers"!

SELF-COMPASSION VERSUS SELF-ESTEEM

In order to define self-compassion I first want to give you some background on compassion. Compassion literally means to "suffer together". Emotionally speaking, compassion is the feeling that arises when you see others suffer and you become intrinsically motivated to alleviate this suffering. Compassion is slightly different from altruism or empathy, even though the concepts are closely related. Empathy relates to our ability to "put ourselves into someone else's shoes", to be able to relate to someone else's feelings. Altruism, a selfless behaviour to help others, often stems from compassion but doesn't necessarily have to be motivated by it. It has been scientifically proven that compassion is deeply rooted in human evolution, and as Dacher Keltner points out in his article "The Compassionate Species", Charles Darwin in *The Descent of Men* had already argued that sympathy might be humanity's strongest instinct, even greater than self-interest. Human babies are the most vulnerable offspring on Earth; they are completely helpless and reliant on their parents and families for a considerable time period. They rely fully on the care, love and compassion of their families in order to survive. Keltner argues that here lies the key to our intrinsic desire to be good and caring, despite the often horrendous behaviour we humans display much too often.

Harvard University in their guidelines to "raising caring children" point out that "research in human development clearly shows that the seeds of empathy, caring and compassion are present from early in life, but that to become caring ethical people, children need adults to help them at every stage of childhood to nurture these seeds into full development." They further argue that "when children can empathise with and take responsibility for others, they are more likely to be happier and more successful. They'll have better relationships their entire lives, and strong relationships are the key ingredient of happiness". Neuroscience shows that the same areas in our brains light up when we experience pain as when we see others suffer pain. Our brains are literally wired to be compassionate.

Self-compassion is an integral part of kindness; it is the kindness, love and understanding towards ourselves. We all know the little grumpy mini-me sitting on our shoulders occasionally bombarding us with these little nuggets of criticism: "Why did you have to do that?", "You should have done this instead," "You won't be good enough anyway," "Why do you always make this mistake?" The list goes on. When we are honest about it, we are our own biggest critic. The relationship with ourselves can be more fraught than with people we have a troublesome or difficult relationship with. We often put ourselves under pressure by our own expectations and criticism. I often have heated discussions with myself, and more often than not they end up making me feel defeated, sad, worthless and self-conscious. Thankfully through the practice of mindfulness I have learned to be more aware of these episodes of self-criticism and "catch" them before the discussion in my head takes off beyond rescue. This is no different for children, and it is vital for their resilience, self-confidence and self-love that we teach our children about self-compassion from an early age.

SELF–ESTEEM: PROCEED WITH CAUTION

There has actually been evidence in recent research that focusing on teaching self-confidence and self-esteem, rather than self-compassion, can have detrimental effects on children and can evolve into narcissistic and over-confident traits that are not helpful for children's development and their behaviour towards others.

Jean M. Twenge, professor of psychology at San Diego State University, and W. Keith Campbell, associate professor of psychology at the University of Georgia, wrote a book in 2010 entitled *The Narcissism Epidemic: Living in the Age of Entitlement*, in which they provide scientific evidence for the connection between the focus on self-esteem and the rise in narcissism. In the late 1960s, a "movement toward self-esteem" started a trend of focusing on artificially teaching self-confidence and self-esteem. This signalled a move away from a more community-oriented way of thinking. Twenge and Campbell also point out that parenting styles changed significantly: away from providing clear rules and limits towards "getting whatever they want". In their book's chapter "Raising Royalty" it is proposed that this development contributed to the rise of narcissism and inflated self-confidence, causing a negative trend in the development of children's mental well-being.

In her article "The role of self-compassion in development – a healthier way to relate to oneself", Kristin D. Neff, associate professor of Human Development and Culture at the University of Texas, suggests that self-esteem is also associated with the so-called "better-than-average effect": the need to feel superior to others in order to feel good about oneself. This would imply that being average is unacceptable in our society. In other words, we have to strive towards the unrealistic picture of perfection all the time. Unfortunately, this "better-than-average effect" not only inflates egos, it also has the nasty side effect of automatically putting others down. According to Neff, this creates interpersonal distance and separation that undermines connectedness. I would myself go so far as to argue that focusing too much on self-esteem and self-confidence is oftentimes a contributing factor to bullying and disrespectful behaviour. Further research shows that, in reality, high self-esteem does not seem to have a positive impact on higher academic or professional performance or improved leadership skills, nor does it prevent addiction issues. High self-esteem also does not prevent behaviours previously associated with low self-esteem such as aggressive and antisocial behaviours.

WHAT IS SELF-COMPASSION?

Dr Kristin Neff (www.self-compassion.org) gives the following three components of what self-compassion is:

1. Self-kindness vs. Self-judgement
Self-compassion entails being warm and understanding toward ourselves when we suffer, fail, or feel inadequate rather than ignoring our pain or flagellating ourselves with self-criticism. Self-compassionate people recognise that being imperfect, failing, and experiencing life difficulties is inevitable, so they tend to be gentle with themselves when confronted with painful experiences rather than getting angry when life falls short of set ideals. People cannot always be or get exactly what they want. When this reality is denied or fought against, suffering increases in the form of stress, frustration and self-criticism. When this reality is accepted with sympathy and kindness, greater emotional equanimity is experienced.

72

2. Common humanity vs. Isolation

Frustration at not having things exactly as we want is often accompanied by an irrational but pervasive sense of isolation – as if "I" were the only person suffering or making mistakes. All humans suffer, however. The very definition of being 'human' means that one is mortal, vulnerable and imperfect. Therefore, self-compassion involves recognising that suffering and personal inadequacy is part of the shared human experience – something that we all go through rather than being something that happens to 'me' alone.

3. Mindfulness vs. Over-identification

Self-compassion also requires taking a balanced approach to our negative emotions so that feelings are neither suppressed nor exaggerated. This equilibrated stance stems from the process of relating personal experiences to those of others who are also suffering, thus putting our own situation into a larger perspective. It also stems from the willingness to observe our negative thoughts and emotions with openness and clarity, so that they are held in mindful awareness. Mindfulness is a non-judgemental, receptive mind state in which one observes thoughts and feelings as they are, without trying to suppress or deny them. We cannot ignore our pain and feel compassion for it at the same time. At the same time, mindfulness requires that we not be 'over-identified' with thoughts and feelings, so that we are caught up and swept away by negative reactivity.

Whereas the teaching of self-esteem and self-confidence in isolation mainly focuses on our "perfection" and "greatness", the teaching of "self-compassion" involves a more realistic view of ourselves. We are not perfect, we will never be, and that's perfectly fine because nobody else is either. Don't get me wrong, I believe self-esteem and self-confidence are very important factors to be nurtured in children, but not at the cost of others and not at the loss of a sense of reality.

I think if we instil in children an unrealistic picture of perfection, the frustration and disappointment when they realise they are not as good as others in certain areas, or they can't achieve a certain goal for whatever reason that may be, will be more damaging than knowing that they can't be fantastic at everything. Self-compassion is strongly linked to psychological well-being and feelings of happiness, optimism, connectedness and curiosity as well as a decrease in depression, anxiety and the fear of failure. It also seems to be the case that increased self-compassion has a positive impact on admitting mistakes, re-evaluating situations and making productive changes as a result. In a classroom setting, it appears that a self-compassionate approach encourages an intrinsically motivated attitude to learning rather than outside pressure. Recent research suggests self-compassion among teens is most successfully fostered and present within a nurturing and supportive family environment with strong attachment and maternal support.

INSTILLING TOLERANCE AND WELCOMING DIVERSITY

Society has never been as diverse as it is today. Difference presents itself at every moment in the shape of one or more of the following: nationality, religion, culture, wealth, gender and sexuality, family structures and, of course, expectations. We are also living in an era of challenging social and political phenomena: the "novel approach" to terrorism, the current refugee crisis, the rise in far-right politics in many Western countries and the varied precarious international political situations. I think never before has it been as important to teach our children the importance of acceptance and tolerance of "difference" in every possible sense. Only if our children learn from a young age to value everybody's humanity before and beyond their differences, will we be able to build an inclusive and peaceful society.

The Oxford Dictionary defines "tolerance" as follows: "The ability or willingness to tolerate the existence of opinions or behaviours that one dislikes or disagrees with."

Webster's New World Dictionary gives this definition: "Tolerance – tolerating or being tolerant, esp. of views, beliefs, practices, etc. of others that differ from one's own; freedom from bigotry or prejudice."

I prefer the second definition, as I believe the key lies in "differences" rather than "dislikes". Everybody probably knows that tolerance and acceptance certainly don't come naturally and easily to us at times. We all have our personal prejudices, misconceptions and generalisations about people, places and cultures. Maybe we are just unfamiliar with them, maybe we have grown up in an environment in which our belief system has been influenced by our families or others, maybe we had a previous experience that had an effect on our point of view; there are many factors that can influence our opinions.

From a young age, children are able to "spot the difference", initially just stating facts as they see them and the truth as they perceive it. We all know the phrase: "Out of the mouth of babes." Our daughters have often landed us in interesting situations to say the least, commenting on peoples' size, nationality, dress, accent … you name it. I remember sitting in the waiting room of the maternity ward when I was expecting our second daughter when my two and a half year old blurted out, "Mama, look at the chocolate man!" She was pointing towards the Nigerian consultant making his way to an expectant mother. There was no ill intention, no prejudice, no racism, just a basic observation. As children get older they pick up on the concept of impropriety by the feedback we give them. They also become gradually more aware of their own and others' looks and abilities. A couple of days ago my older daughter, who is naturally tall and skinny, commented on her little sister's body as they were putting on their pyjamas. "You are fat," she simply said. She wasn't teasing, she was just stating a fact that arose from a comparison to her own body shape. Of course I jumped straight to my little girl's defence, which instantly changed the dynamic. Her big sister took on a teasing tone straight away, pushing the little one's buttons as she knew she was on to something. It was through my reaction this happened, and I instantly knew it. Rather than getting further annoyed with my older daughter I just tried to defuse the situation by distraction, which worked eventually, but it was the perfect example of how intolerance and being negative about differences can start so easily if we're not mindful.

Oftentimes it can be out of our control what children pick up from others in relation to prejudices and judgements, especially when they start school and other activities outside the home. It's only a normal part of growing up that children "get to know" the viewpoints of their peers and other people in their environment. It's not always easy though to realise that it's not just us anymore who influence our children's thinking and beliefs. We all want to fit in and feel accepted. Children are no different, and in order to do so they will go along with their peers' opinions and even deny their true feelings and beliefs just to be part of a group. This can be as harmless as joining in with games they don't really enjoy or pretending they love the same comics or movies as the others even if they don't. Unfortunately it doesn't always stay so innocent, and it can evolve into negatively influencing beliefs and viewpoints or even bullying if the child doesn't conform or "fit in". We have all experienced peer pressure at some point in our lives, and it can be so hard to be our true self, especially when we are that little bit "different" from the majority. I still clearly remember this terrible feeling of not fitting in, not being part of anything in my primary school years. We lived in a small village where many people were related; most children had a couple of cousins in their class and probably more within the school. We were the only family that wasn't originally from the area, and even though I don't remember severe bullying, I was always made to feel that I wasn't really a part of "it" in one way or another. I recall my efforts to fit in – it even went so far as me being the only member of my family speaking the local dialect! The teachers at the time weren't very supportive or even "clued in", and as I never felt "safe" or "comfortable" in school I would often have tummy aches in the morning. Thankfully primary school in Germany only lasts four years, and everything changed once I started secondary school in the bigger town nearby, where there was a mix of children from various villages. This period in secondary school was mostly a positive experience, and I made many lifelong friends. During this time I learned a lot about tolerance and acceptance. We had great camaraderie amongst the pupils, and some fantastic teachers encouraged fairness, tolerance and an open-minded view to life. Our well-loved religion teacher, despite being an ordained priest, taught us with a very inclusive, critical and tolerant attitude about the more precarious elements and views of the Catholic church on issues like contraception, celibacy or outdated church laws.

In fairness, we are often pushed to our very limits even when we try very hard to be tolerant. I can understand when people are nervous and even fearful when confronted with unknown and somewhat threatening situations. One recent example is the badly managed resettling of refugees into small rural and close-knit communities, often without proper preparation and transparent information. Would I be happy if there were twenty strange men housed beside my child's primary school with short notice and no further explanation? No, I certainly wouldn't. Tolerance to me can only be achieved with appropriate education, transparent information and very importantly being sensitive to people's fears and worries.

Bulgarian politician and Director-General of UNESCO, Irina Bokova, powerfully stated in March 2014:

> Respect and tolerance are liberating acts, whereby the differences of others are recognised as the same as our own and whereby the riches of another culture are taken as the wealth of all.

The UNESCO website gives the following recommendation on promoting tolerance:

> Along with outright injustice and violence, discrimination and marginalization are common forms of intolerance. Education for tolerance should aim at countering influences that lead to fear and exclusion of others, and should help young people develop capacities for independent judgement, critical thinking and ethical reasoning. The diversity of our world's many religions, languages, cultures and ethnicities is not a pretext for conflict, but is a treasure that enriches us all.
>
> On the day of its fiftieth anniversary, 16 November 1995, UNESCO's Member States adopted a Declaration of Principles on Tolerance. Among other things, the Declaration affirms that tolerance is neither indulgence nor indifference. It is respect and appreciation of the rich variety of our world's cultures, our forms of expression and ways of being human. Tolerance recognises the universal human rights and fundamental freedoms of others. People are naturally diverse; only tolerance can ensure the survival of mixed communities in every region of the globe.

I am of the firm belief that the root of intolerant, offensive or aggressive behaviour is very often the fear of the unknown and ignorance in its true sense. It is our responsibility as educators and parents to teach our children about the differences in our society and that it is perfectly fine to be different. Not only will this help to build more tolerance, it will also let our children know that they are okay just the way they are, including the differences they might present with. As with any other area, we need to start at the "bottom" rather than confront them with threatening global issues: some people are big, others are small; some people wear glasses, others need a wheelchair; some children are great at sports, others are amazing little artists; some boys like pink, some girls love playing with trucks and tractors.

My personal motto on tolerance is: "As long as we don't harm others or ourselves with our differences, it's all good." We don't all need to blend into homogenous groups – how boring would that be? Differences make our society colourful, vibrant and interesting and we should embrace them in ourselves and others.

SO, IN PRACTICAL TERMS, HOW CAN WE INSTIL TOLERANCE?

I recently read a lovely article about the wording around the issue of tolerance in relation to a diverse and multicultural society. The related verb "to tolerate", as stated in this article, makes it sound as if people of a different nationality or culture are like "bugs in a picnic". It doesn't have a very positive ring to it. Undoubtedly, we need to re-evaluate the terminology as well as the definition of tolerance. The article suggested replacing "tolerating" with "celebrating" – an altogether finer choice of verb.

Our lives can be so enriched when we get to know the traditions, foods, music, literature, dress and history of other cultures and nationalities. An excellent first step as parents and teachers is to create an awareness of all the "foreign" things that are already a part of our everyday lives: check the labels of our clothing, where was it made? Where does your favourite food like pizza, spaghetti, curry or tacos come from originally? Where does your favourite musician come from? Where was your favourite movie filmed? Hang up a map of the world and mark with a pin whenever you find something else that affects you regularly. You will be amazed how many pins end up on the map. You could have themed mealtimes and celebrations either at home or in school: an Italian ristorante, Chinese New Year Celebrations, a Mexican fiesta, a Middle Eastern mezze feast. Let children bring in authentic traditional props or clothes such as chopsticks, serving dishes or national dress. If there are children from different cultural backgrounds in the class or group, it is especially fascinating for everyone to experience their friends' traditions, foods, celebrations and music. As a child, my favourite programmes on television were documentaries about how people lived in different parts of our planet. To this day I am fascinated about different cultures, their traditions and history, their celebrations and customs. Young children are inquisitive and free of prejudice and judgement. Using an informal approach, we should encourage and provide an education about how children grow up around the world. There are books, television programmes and webpages readily available. We can integrate an open-minded approach naturally into daily life rather than singling things out. This can be applied to all of our differences: nationality, religion, culture, disability/ability, sexual orientation, family structure etc. My oldest daughter regularly comes home from school with questions like: "Can two girls get married?", "Why does — not take part in religious education?", "Why is — in a wheelchair?", "Why does — Daddy live in a different house?", "Why did the lady on the telly wear a cloth over her head?" Most parents are familiar with these or similar questions, and we all know that some of them can be challenging to answer. Rather than changing the subject, we should try to be prepared to answer these questions in an age-appropriate and truthful manner.

I believe the more open we are about differences with our children and students in school, the more normal and integrated they are for them growing up. From a young age, my two girls have been watching a programme on Cbeebies called "Mr Tumble". It is a children's programme involving a clown called Mr Tumble, his family and children with varying disabilities. Young viewers are introduced to "Makaton" sign language, which is naturally integrated into the programme. They both love it, and it very naturally introduced them to different disabilities. They have always asked loads of questions and we have always tried to answer them as best we could. Our general approach in our chats is: "Everybody is different; everybody is unique."

As a teacher and parent of children with special needs, I believe that children with special needs should not be treated with undue attention or lowered expectations. We just need to make sure resources and supports are in place to ensure children are able to access the curriculum within an appropriate placement. In a classroom environment it should be a given to include experiences and materials that naturally include people with various disabilities not only directly related to the children with a disability in class.

Invite outside speakers with disabilities not necessarily focusing on the disability, but on their job, sport, hobbies etc. to illustrate that disabilities don't mean people can't reach their goals or find their place in society.

We probably all need a few lessons every so often in being comfortable speaking about tolerance and about differences. Let's be honest, some topics are easier to address than others. If we are not comfortable answering questions in an honest and understandable way, children will pick this up, which will add to the confusion about things they are not familiar with. There is no shame in saying, "I don't know the answer to this. Let's find a book about it or research it on the internet." We don't have all the answers, but as long as we keep an open mind and a willingness to engage in educating our children, it's all good. I have included some practical games and exercises for both home and school in Part Two.

Chapter 7

The need for change in our primary school education system

"LEARNING–BY–DOING"

I trained as a primary school teacher in Germany nearly twenty-five years ago. The old-fashioned teaching methodology of "frontal instruction" – children sitting at their benches listening to the teacher's instructions and mostly using only books and copies – was only a small part of the school day in primary schools at the time and in the schools I trained in. Children were encouraged to follow the approach of "learning-by-doing", where writing, reading and maths were integrated into different projects rather than done for the sake of it. A project I did during my training serves as an example of how this approach was carried out: we introduced the topic "forest" as a framework for all parts of the curriculum for a couple of weeks for six- and seven-year-old students. Firstly we took the children on a day-long expedition to the forest to immerse them into the experience. They were given small tasks involving all the senses: what sounds can you hear? What does it smell like? Which colours can you see? Did you see any animals? As it was summertime they waded through a little stream and felt the texture of the soil with their bare feet. Over the subsequent days, all subjects were integrated into the topic: songs and rhymes about the forest, art activities using materials from the forest, counting and writing down artefacts collected on our trip (e.g. four pine cones, six acorns, seven pebbles, two twigs). The children did activities such as laying pebbles or twigs in the shapes of letters or numbers; the possibilities were endless. At the end of the project we had an exhibition for the rest of the school and the children's parents, which was a positive and motivating conclusion to two weeks of work.

When following the "learning-by-doing" approach, children don't even notice they are doing their writing, reading and maths, as the activities are meaningful and motivating. They are also, dare I even say it, great fun. Emphasis is put on working with a partner or in teams, sharing and dividing materials fairly and doing activities independently. Once the task is finished, children bring it to the "finished" table and start a new activity. Children can move around freely while following respectful rules. This ensures productive work without too much disturbance. For children that finish work a bit earlier, areas are set up where they can either do further reading or activities, or even play games around the project topic. Students' self-confidence flourishes as they are proud of their achievements and delighted they are trusted to work independently. Even though this system requires a lot of preparation for the teacher beforehand, once the project is set up, the teacher is able to observe and help individual children that might require a little bit of extra support. Also, materials are differentiated in a way that doesn't make it obvious to the students that a particular child might be a little slower or have difficulties reading or writing etc.

Teaching in Ireland, and possibly in other European countries, is being hindered by an inappropriate amount of formal testing and record keeping. I don't believe that young children should have to be put through formal assessment at all unless there are serious concerns about psychological or developmental issues. Why should there be checklists in pre-school and early primary school to record every small step? Teachers know their students and their learning style and needs, and continuous assessment takes place all the time as an integral part of teaching. It takes precious time away from getting fully immersed into a more wholesome style of teaching and learning. Of course there needs to be assessment at some stage, but not in this constant manner that makes teachers and students uncomfortable in their classrooms and puts unnecessary pressure on everybody. I believe it sends out the wrong message to children from an early age: that we have to live up to a certain standard, that we are not good enough, that we should strive to be better than someone else. I am amazed how it is still okay to have a Leaving Certificate that solely relies on the results of the exams. What about all the work students have put in throughout the years? It is proven that students perform differently when put under severe pressure and some even falter. Naturally children have to prepare for a life in which they will have to make an effort to achieve something, but there should be fairness and an appreciation for all the work done throughout the school year.

In my opinion and experience, children learn maths, reading and writing at their own pace and flourish if they are supported in their natural learning style. Some children learn best with visual support, some find it easier to learn through practical actions, some just need to listen to retain information easily – every child is different and a learning style does not define a child's intelligence. If we don't make things motivating and meaningful and respect individual learning styles and abilities, we will instil frustration, low self-esteem and unhealthy competitive behaviours. When children feel supported and understood in school, this will have a positive ripple effect on other areas. My older daughter finds school a little challenging to say the least. She is okay following the curriculum and doesn't have major problems following lessons, but she doesn't really enjoy much of the school work, which sometimes I can understand. Luckily she has a wonderful teacher who takes the initiative and puts in a lot of effort. The fact that she likes her a lot makes things much easier also. She came home from school one day not too long ago with her homework and as usual it was our daily struggle to get started. One part of her homework was to write the sentence "I like big ships" three times in her workbook. She looked at me and said, "Mama, why do I have to write this? I don't like big ships." Looking back, I am actually mad that I insisted on her doing the exercise, as I fully agreed with her sentiment. Yes, children should learn that sometimes they have to do things they don't necessarily love, but why can't the majority of content be more motivating?

Children find it so much easier to follow meaningful instructions such as, write a shopping list, an invitation or a letter. It is not that difficult to make these changes and move away from the current rigid approach. Even though we have a good core curriculum, it needs to become firmly embedded within a change in priorities for our children's well-being and delivered through more flexible and child-centred methodologies. Rather than sitting still and following the teacher's instructions for the majority of the school day, children should be encouraged to learn by working in pairs and groups and even to explore curriculum content independently within a structured set-up. Music, art, experiential approaches and outdoor activities should have a much higher priority in primary schools rather than focusing mainly on reading, writing and maths. Again, if it is properly integrated it's not a matter of either/or. Children don't even realise that they are learning academic content when it is taught through a more creative, active and musical approach. "Learning-by-doing" has been proven to support learning for hundreds of years. When children experience a subject, get fully immersed and can experiment in a safe environment to see first-hand how things work, education becomes an adventure and encourages children to want to learn more.

THE VALUE OF HOMEWORK

At the danger of getting myself into real trouble, I believe that homework should consist of no more than a short, ten-minute activity or even better, should be abandoned altogether, especially during the first four years of primary school. Children spend most of their day in school. Depending on their bus journeys and the time of year there is barely any time left to even just kick a ball for a few minutes without even doing any homework. I dare to say that there is absolutely no educational benefit in homework for young children in primary school, and in most families, including my own, it causes frustration, stress and confrontation. That doesn't mean that children shouldn't be encouraged to read at home; for me, reading does not really fall into the category of homework, it is a life skill and a source of joy and excitement, and it is our responsibility as parents and educators to instil a love for books.

Up to this point, I have presented my personal experience and opinion. However, for the purpose of this chapter, I have researched some scientific views on this topic. In his 2015 article "Does homework help or hinder young children?" Gerald K. LeTendre suggests that there is no evidence to show that homework for young children is of academic benefit. On the contrary, studies have actually linked excessive homework to sleep disruption and stress for young children. The Duke University professor, Harris Cooper, found evidence in his 2006 study that even though there is a positive correlation between homework and student achievement for older students, i.e. secondary school students, this relationship is weak for young children in primary schools. Cathy Vatterott, an education professor at the University of Missouri St. Louis, thinks there is no sufficient proof that homework is of any benefit for primary school students and she supports efforts to eliminate homework for young children.

THE FINNISH EXAMPLE

If we look at the education system in Finland for example, which time and time again has been recognised as one of the best school systems in the world, there are some very crucial differences in their approach to teaching young children to the education system in Ireland and many other Western countries. (Pisa studies verify the success of the Finnish education system with the last one conducted in 2012.) In Finland, formal education doesn't start until the children are seven years of age, as it is believed that children are not mature enough before that and need their early childhood to be imaginative, to be creative, to have a certain amount of freedom, to be physically active – to just be a child! The main aim of education in the early years is the children's health and well-being. Children learn to develop good social habits, make friends and respect themselves and others. They learn basic life skills such as dressing and self-care. A big emphasis lies on physical outdoor activity. In short, the aim of early childhood education is to make sure that

children develop into happy and responsible individuals who can then concentrate on a more academic schooling without losing sight of all other aspects.

This approach is anything but random; even though activities are play based, children's development is constantly evaluated. Play varies from free play to teacher-assisted play, activities are carefully planned and the aim is learning through play. Play helps children to become powerful learners, according to David Whitebread, director of the Centre for Research on Play in Education, Development & Learning at the University of Cambridge. In his professional opinion, carefully organised play helps develop qualities such as attention span, perseverance, concentration and problem solving, which at the age of four are stronger predictors of academic success than the age at which a child learns to read or write. There is evidence that good early-years, play-based learning not only supports educational development but boosts attainment in children from disadvantaged areas who mightn't have the cultural background enjoyed by their wealthier peers. Whitebread states, "The better the quality of pre-school, the better the outcomes, both emotionally and socially and in terms of academic achievement."

The Finnish National Board of Education says unashamedly that the heart of the education system is the "joy of learning". Their website states that:

> The objective of basic education is to support pupils' growth towards humanity and ethically responsible membership of society and to provide them with the knowledge and skills needed in life.

> The focus in education is on learning rather than testing. There are no national tests for pupils in basic education in Finland. Instead, teachers are responsible for assessment in their respective subjects on the basis of the objectives included in the curriculum.

You might wonder why I am talking about an education system that has nothing to do with ours. Well, that is exactly the point I am trying to make. Whether it concerns the health system, the education system or any other vital department, I cannot understand why, if we know in theory how it should be done by paying attention to the countries that have proven to be successful in a certain area, is it not possible to take on board their expertise and make the necessary changes? We need to get more involved and active in the decision making that has such a significant impact on our children. We need to voice our concerns and worries, come up with suggestions and solutions and support positive change. All of us – parents, educators, politicians, responsible members of our society – we all need to work together and support each other to achieve necessary and positive changes in our education system. Let's do it!

Chapter 8

The internet, social media and screens:
a modern-day challenge

If you asked me what I believe is the biggest challenge, even curse, of our time in relation to raising children, I would have to answer: the internet, social media and smartphones. Even though our two daughters are both under six, I am already dreading the day when I won't be able to control the influence of these devices. The issue is complex, has no easy answers and is problematic not only for children and teenagers but for adults also. The next time you go into a café or restaurant take note of the amount of people around you who are using a smartphone. Believe me when I tell you it is a shocking exercise to do. There is no denying the fantastic advantages and opportunities offered by "Mr Google". The ease of access to information today is literally a game-changer. However, the ever-increasing reliance on if not addiction to our smartphones is worrying. It presents a clear threat to our real-world presence and in particular social connections and relationships. We are often not even aware of the "real people" around us anymore because we are focused on connecting to others on Facebook, Twitter or Snapchat. From a mindfulness point of view there is another aspect to this problem, as Dr Dan Siegel addresses in his book *Brainstorm*:

> And while there are a lot of great connections we can make through social media that enhance friendship and social connections in general, the danger is that we fail to pay attention to other aspects of our lives. Hours and days can go by without our taking time-in to just be with our inner life.

If we direct our attention outwards and into cyberspace for extended periods of time, we are not present in this very moment and the surrounds we find ourselves in. We will have little awareness of our inner world, our thoughts, emotions and even physical sensations. We detach from the real world, from real people and from ourselves.

Due to various circumstances children are spending too much time in front of screens: the television, gaming consoles, tablets, computers and smartphones. I think it has taken on the dimensions of an addiction, and children are becoming increasingly disconnected from the real world. There are many studies suggesting that, especially in the first three years of a child's life, the so-called "critical period", permanent damage can be done to brain development by too much exposure to "screen time". A young child needs certain stimuli from their environment and the people in it. "Real-world" stimuli are crucial for brain development and cannot be replicated in activities on tablets or smartphones. The overuse of these devices can lead to the stunting of development in certain areas of the brain. When young children are read stories by their parents for example, it encourages their brain to imagine parts of the storyline: what the characters in the story might look like, where they live, what their voices might sound like. Screens take away this process, as it spoon-feeds the total experience. This will actually make children's imaginations lazy and weaken their cognitive muscles.

During this crucial early-childhood period, the frontal lobe is developing. This part of the brain is responsible for understanding and decoding social interactions and non-verbal communication such as tone of voice, gestures, facial expressions and body movements which form a significant part of social communication. The frontal lobe is responsible for enabling us to empathise with others and read vital cues of social communication. In short, it enables us to form relationships, communicate and read social situations appropriately. This development will only happen through real-life interactions, and if children miss out on these interactions due to the overuse of devices, these empathic abilities might be impaired forever, which, according to psychologist Dr Liraz Margalit, would have a significantly detrimental effect on their lives.

Dr Aric Sigman, an associate fellow of the British Psychological Society and a Fellow of Britain's Royal Society of Medicine, says:

Too much screen time too soon is the very thing impeding the development of the abilities that parents are so eager to foster through the tablets. The ability to focus, to concentrate, to lend attention, to sense other people's attitudes and communicate with them, to build a large vocabulary—all those abilities are harmed.

Children and teenagers are increasingly presenting with near-obsessive use of their smartphone or tablet, especially in relation to social connections. There is rarely a group of kids or teenagers to be seen chatting without at least one of them looking at a phone. As a result, children are missing out on real-life social and communication skills and the ability to connect the old-fashioned way. We all know that we communicate differently when we are behind a screen or phone as opposed to talking face-to-face. Excessive screen time also affects the pursuit of activities and hobbies, which, in turn, also diminishes real-life social connections.

This disconnect, I believe, is responsible for new forms of inappropriate communication, such as cyberbullying, sexting, obsession with selfies and presenting an unrealistic and false identity due to both peer pressure and opportunity. It is much easier to be cruel behind a screen or say things we wouldn't if we were talking to someone face-to-face. Cruelty and lies thrive with the distance behind the screen. Social media is often used to "shame" children and teenagers (and grown-ups too) and could involve videos that were filmed secretly or pictures taken in private situations. When we were teenagers we all did some silly things, but now every little mistake or embarrassing moment is captured forever and circulated for maximum "shaming". Even the ever-present possibility of these practices must influence teenagers' behaviour, demeanour, self-confidence and authenticity. I can only imagine the level of discomfort and distrust that exists when living in the knowledge that every step I take, every word I say could possibly be broadcast to a large audience at the click of a button. This must have a significant influence on the way teenagers present themselves, and I suspect that many interactions lack true authenticity and comfort with who they really are. Young teenage girls especially feel unrelenting pressure to conform to certain beauty and body images promoted by the media, and in particular social media. Unrealistic expectations put great pressure on these vulnerable girls to look and act a certain way.

For me personally, one of the scariest aspects of smartphones and internet access is that teenagers and children have unsupervised access to anything online. They are exposed to extremely graphic content on a regular basis without having the maturity to process and understand what they are confronted with. As a result, I believe there is a warped understanding of what is normal and acceptable. Kids are vulnerable to online predators who have the opportunity of constant and easy access, often hiding behind fake profiles of peers. We as parents have no way of controlling this unless we put our children on constant supervision, which is obviously unrealistic.

I used to think, and sometimes still do, that there should be legislation around the use and ownership of smartphones, but as we all know too well, this would probably not solve the issue at hand and could potentially make it worse. As with most challenges, I believe that education is the key; it's the only way to even attempt to tackle the influence of social media and the internet in general has on our generation of children and teenagers. Unfortunately I know that many of us parents, including myself, often try and ignore the severity of possible threats this area poses to our children. I had a discussion with my principal a few days ago about this very topic and we agreed that parents need "shock therapy" in order to "wake up" and become aware of what our children and teenagers are exposed to at the click of a button, and it won't be a pretty sight.

Imagine the scenario of googling the following: paedophile, porn, child pornography. I can say, with a hand on my heart, that I would be much too terrified to do this. The abyss of horror into which I could fall petrifies me, and I am an adult with the ability to judge my own decisions and the consequences thereafter. Children are developmentally not able to process the graphic contents they are regularly confronted with, but due to easy access, peer pressure and their own natural curiosity they are experiencing a "reality" that I am sure would knock the socks off some of us grown-ups! I mentioned the Channel 4 programme *The Sex Education Show* before and the secondary-school survey conducted to inform parents about what their children are exposed to online in relation to porn and violence. The reaction of the parents said it all. The effects of inappropriate content have already started to severely affect our children. We see more and more inappropriate sexual and violent behaviours, a rise in bullying and teenage suicides and new methods of predators targeting children online. That's the tip of the iceberg. We can't close our eyes any longer, at least not to the reality of this extremely difficult challenge of our times. We need to educate ourselves and our children about the reality and the dangers in a very open-minded and upfront manner.

This is what I believe we as parents can do to support our children and prepare them for the responsible use of technology:

- Be a good role model: we have all fallen into the smart-phone trap. Try and model the behaviour you want your kids to adopt. Set certain times aside to check your emails, Facebook messages etc. Maybe the best time would be when the children have either left the house or gone to bed. Set an example and spend your time as a family face-to-face, and limit technology wherever possible.

- Limit the use of tablets, television and smartphones for young children under three in particular to less than one hour a day. Make sure young children are supervised at all times when using the internet.

- Spend quality time together as a family and promote outdoor activities.

- Support and encourage your children's interests, encourage social outings, such as sports, scouts, drama groups etc.

- Build up trust. Our children need to know that we trust them rather than us stalking our older children's Face-book profile, for example. This trust will also ensure that our children will tell us if they are being targeted by peers or others in an inappropriate manner, or if they have access to inappropriate content via friends or school mates when we are not present.

- Stay informed! We have to have regular honest and frank conversations with our children concerning the dangers of the internet and social media. If we are not comfort-able to discuss things in detail, organise talks in school or other groups by experts who know how to explain and answer questions (i.e. guards, psychologists, teachers, social workers etc.) We also have to make an effort to stay informed about new trends, games and crazes in order to bring them up in conversation with our children and discuss them.

- Encourage and model the aforementioned traits of kindness, tolerance, compassion and self-compassion. They are as valid, or even more so, in relation to interactions on social media.

Chapter 9

The importance of play

The most important "mindfulness exercise" you will ever do with your child is play.

Y ou may find this strange, but I feel we all need to be reminded sometimes about the meaning of play. The following seems to be at the core of most definitions:

Play: A physical or mental leisure activity that is undertaken purely for enjoyment or amusement and has no other objective.

Much more than adults, children are able to deeply connect with what they are doing. They immerse themselves so completely into their play that they can forget everything around them. Through play, children not only connect fully with their activity, they also connect with themselves and make happy experiences through autonomous discoveries and creations. These experiences are stored and lead to the growth of the neuro-network in their brain that is activated during these moments, transmitting feelings of joy about their "doing" and happiness about themselves. Grown-ups can sometimes catch a precious glimpse of this mental state when pursuing activities that get our full devotion and passion, such as playing an instrument, painting, cooking or baking. These activities can make us forget the time and keep us in the here and now with no thoughts about the past or future. It's these short moments that give us a feeling of freedom and happiness, of connectedness with ourselves and the present moment and a little taste of "child's play".

Children's imaginations are incredible, and I am always blown away by the endless possibilities they seem to find to engage in meaningful play even without the presence of toys or games. My daughters' favourite "toys" for as long as I can remember have been cardboard boxes, my clothes, blankets, pillows and chairs. With those they have travelled into space and to every country known to them; they have built buses, airplanes, huts and houses, nests and caves. They have cared for their babies or treated patients in hospital. A child will always find possibilities to play, even in the most deprived corners of the world. My husband and I went on a holiday to South Africa a few years ago and I remember meeting this little boy pushing a little car made from rusty wire and plastic bottle tops. He was completely immersed in an imaginary race and as happy as could be. This image had a profound effect on me and has stayed with me ever since. It was the living proof that play is not an activity or a choice but an integral part of our development and of our "being human".

One of my favourite films ever made is *Babies*, a 2006 documentary by Thomas Balmes. It follows four mothers and their babies from birth for one year. The mothers lived in Opuwo, rural Namibia, Bayanchandmani, rural Mongolia, Tokyo, Japan and San Francisco, USA. I was in awe of the differences in their experiences, attitudes, environmental and social factors, especially the two mothers from very remote corners of the world. At one point, the Mongolian mum hopped on her husband's motorbike with the baby tied to her body, only hours after giving birth in what I very much doubt could have been termed even a hospital. What really struck me though was not the differences, but the similarities of the children's development, especially their natural need for play. The environments and toys may have been very different, but all four children developed their skills similarly. It was one of the most fascinating documentaries I have ever seen and I would recommend it to anybody who has even the slightest interest in child development or even just an interest in how people live in different parts of the world.

Play is a fundamental right and need of all children. Play as a childhood *right* has been set in stone within the United Nations Convention on the Rights of the Child (UNCRC) since 1989. The stated intention of the UNCRC with respect to play and recreation is to assure to all the world's children the benefit of a satisfying play life. In the following few paragraphs I will give a little more formal, research-backed evidence to the importance of play.

THE RESEARCH OF PLAY

When the American psychologist and educator David Elkind, whose work is mostly based on the research of Jean Piaget, first wrote his book *The Hurried Child* in response to what he perceived even then as the increasing pressures in a changing society on children to grow up quickly and the consequential stress on children, he concluded that "in the end, a childhood is the most basic right of children". Twenty-five years later, commenting on the greater appreciation of the importance of free, self-initiated and spontaneous play to the child's healthy, mental, emotional and social development, Elkind emphasises that, "in the end, a **playful childhood** is the most basic right of childhood". In his book, *The Power of Play,* Elkind elaborates on some of the topics that have fascinated him throughout his career.

> I came to see that the unintended side effect of hurrying is silencing children's play ... There are more and more organised activities, and spontaneous play is now seen as a luxury that is not affordable in a high-tech, globalized society. The role of play needed to be clarified: It's a form of learning. Piaget said—and I quote him in the book—that play is the answer to the question, 'How does anything new come about?'

In his report on the value of children's play "The Importance of

Play", Dr David Whitebread illustrates a similar belief with some very interesting research evidence by various authors:

Much of the contemporary work on children's play within developmental psychology is based on the influential theories of the Russian psychologist of the first part of the twentieth century, Lev Vygotsky (1896–1934). His writings were not published in English until the 1970s as Stalin's dictatorship suppressed his work. Since the publications his ideas about the processes of children's learning have been enormously influential. The major insight as regards the role of play (Vygotsky, 1978) was that it makes two crucial contributions to children's developing abilities, which relate to their development of language, verbal and non-verbal, and to their abilities of cognitive and emotional self-regulation. There is overwhelming evidence that language development and the ability to self-regulate are closely inter-related and that they may be the most precise predictors of a child's academic development and emotional and mental well-being.

Psychologist Jerome Bruner highlighted the long-held recognition that, through evolution, as more and more complex animals evolved, the size of their brains increased, and this was associated with increasingly longer periods of biological immaturity (i.e. the length of time the young were cared for by their parents), paralleled by increasing playfulness. There seems to be a strong and consistent relationship between children's playfulness and their cognitive and emotional development.

In her research paper "Play as a context for Early Learning and Development", commissioned by the National Council for Curriculum and Assessment, NCCA (Dublin), Margaret Kernan presents some very insightful key points about adult involvement in play:

Considering the role of adults in children's play
Whilst the tendency to play is universally acknowledged as being innate, increasingly it is recognised that in order for play to flourish as a truly enjoyable, cognitive, and socially adaptive human ability, adult support is necessary (Singer, 2006). Identifying the precise form and function of that support however, is not easy. In many cultures and communities, parents are young children's first co-players (Rogoff, 2003). Referring to the importance of parents' interest, enjoyment

97

and involvement in their children's play, Bettelheim (1987) notes that it makes a vast difference to the child and his play if he/she can share his/her experiences with an adult who is able to remember childhood experiences around the same kind of play. Patience and timing are critical in parent–child interactions in play. It is important for parents to provide the physical and mental space to children to play with ideas and materials in ways that are most meaningful to them [the children], and not impose their ideas [the parent's ideas] regarding the 'proper' way to play (Bettelheim, 1987).

"Play" has changed significantly for our children in the last few decades due to many different factors including changing living environments and social situations, changes in health and safety regulations, the rise of technology and its effect on the development of toys, increased affluence, and influenced by these and other factors a change in parenting styles and formal education in schools. As mentioned before most of my childhood experiences around play were unsupervised and child-led i.e. we were let out of the house in the afternoon and returned at a certain agreed time in the evening. This could be extended during holiday time and there were days when we didn't even come home for lunch. We had a limited amount of toys, probably a couple of cuddly toys, a doll and mainly games that could be played with a group of children or the whole family after that. We learned to form our own "mini community", to sort out our differences, to stand our ground, to share and co-operate, to organise ourselves for our mainly outdoor adventures. Children nowadays get very little opportunity to "socialise" without constant adult supervision and in my opinion this is to the detriment of our children's development of crucial social skills. Unfortunately some modern day conditions don't allow the extent of the freedom and flexibility, I would even call it a luxury, that most of us parents and educators might have experienced in our own childhood. We need to make sure though that we still afford our children the opportunities to play and interact with peers without us looking over their shoulders and observing every move, ready to pounce and intervene should there be the slightest sign of a disagreement between them. Children also need to have the time and possibility to just play and occupy themselves on their own, without our interference, unless of course there is an emergency and our support is needed. Playing is learning and through experimenting, exploring and trial and error children learn essential skills "first hand" rather than mostly prescribed and taught by us parents or educators.

Chapter 10

The human need to connect with nature and the outdoors

*The young human needs his own kind —
namely animals, anything elementary,
water, dirt, ditches, room to play.
It's possible to let him grow up without all of this,
with carpets, cuddly toys or on tarmac streets and yards too.
He'll survive, but we should not be surprised if he is unable, in later life,
to learn basic social skills.*

TRANSLATION FROM GERMAN, ALEXANDER MITSCHERLICH,
PSYCHO-ANALYST 1908-1982

s touched on briefly before, our society and children's lives have changed considerably and at a very fast pace over the past fifty years. Sadly, basic experiences, such as unsupervised play and a close connection to nature and the seasons, are increasingly a thing of the past. Like most people of my generation, my own early childhood memories mainly relate to outdoor experiences: meeting friends in the street or forest to play, building dens and tree houses, foraging for berries, mushrooms and nuts, ice skating on the nearby pond, having snowball fights, cycling my bike to visit a friend in the next village, swimming in the stream, rearing frogs from tadpoles and picking and eating wild cherries and strawberries. Even as I write, I can see the health and safety warnings flash in big red letters in my mind! Although I understand a lot of the reservations we have in our modern society, it makes me very sad to see how many children are deprived of these precious and basic experiences. Even within health and safety regulations, we as parents and educators have to make sure that our children can still immerse themselves in outdoor play; it is a fundamental part of childhood and growing up. Children learn from a very early age that our environment is threatened by various, mostly man-made, problems. They are aware that species are endangered and our planet is on the brink of catastrophe. This awareness is yet another source of stress and worry for them.

This theoretical knowledge often stands in stark contrast to the limited actual connection to nature, to direct experience, enjoyment and sensory immersion in all that nature and the outdoors has to offer. My six-year-old daughter came home the other day from school and freaked out when I rinsed my hands under the tap. She shouted at me, "Mama, turn off the tap quick, otherwise the polar bears are going to die!" I am not denying the severe threats to our Earth, but children should be able to actively be part of their environment, rather than worrying about issues that are far too abstract and overwhelming at a young age. Children should learn respect and love for their surroundings from the root, from direct experience. There is plenty of time to learn about a more global outlook.

To be honest, before I started writing this book, I never paid too much attention to the developmental, educational and even evolutional importance of outdoor connections to humans. It was just a status quo for me, the way I grew up, the way it should be for everybody. Sure, in my studies to become a teacher I came across the work of educators and philosophers such as Jean-Jacques Rousseau, Henry David Thoreau and John Dewey, who were probably the first promoters, even founders, of experiential and outdoor education, but still the "real" importance only occurred to me quite recently, probably influenced by both my profession as well as becoming a parent. It was mostly the realisation that for many children nowadays, outdoor play and experiences aren't a natural or regular part of their lives any more. Richard Louv calls this modern phenomenon "Nature-Deficit-Disorder", although he points out that at this stage this is not an actual existing medical diagnosis.

In his book, *Kinder raus!* (translation: *Kids outside!*) Malte Roeper illustrates the intrinsic ancient connection of us humans to the outdoors, which remains to this day, as follows:

> Why are we modern humans touched by this strange emotion when we finally sit down at an open fire? This calming feeling, where does it come from? We sit, stare into the blaze and think: All is good ... This warmth, the flickering of the flames ... We throw the next branch into the flames and know: We did the right thing. Can you remember your last night by an open fire? Was it enjoyable or not? We have long forgotten, but deep within us we are still familiar and connected: To sit at a fire even centuries ago meant safety,

protection, comfort. When our ancestors sat by a fire it usually meant a break in tough times and living conditions, a social event, food. In short 'All is good.' A lot of these connections to different sensory experiences and our emotional reactions are rooted deep within us without us being aware of it. Why is it most desirable to live up on a height? Because it used to be the safest place. Why do we often like to have ponds, wells or pools in our gardens? Because it used to be a luxury to have drinking water close by. Why do children practice imitating animal sounds from a young age? Because it used to be necessary for hunting.

Research shows that when given the opportunity and choice, young children will still opt for outdoor play most of the time. Margaret Kernan, in her aforementioned 2007 research paper, states that it is important to have a good understanding of the meaning of play activities from the perspectives of children in order to be able to provide adequate play opportunities for children. She consulted multiple international studies and when asked about their play activities and preferences, most

participating children in the various studies emphasised their preference for outdoor play among other important factors.

In their book *Wie Kinder heute wachsen – Natur als Entwicklungsraum (How children grow today – Nature as an environment / room for development)*, Herbert Renz-Polster, a paediatrician and scientist, and Gerald Huether, professor for neurobiology, speak right from my heart when they say that for children and their development, nature is not "optional", it's as essential as a healthy diet for growing up. Only in nature and the outdoors do they encounter all four non-negotiable sources for their development: freedom, immediacy, resistance and relatedness (connection). Children have an innate desire to connect with nature. They will strive towards it even in the most horrendous circumstances as the following example shows: In a report about "everyday life" in Mogadishu by Michael Obert, a small boy with a nasty scar on his forehead is seen to water a little tree on the side of the road. The water is trickling through a hole in a plastic bag. When asked about it he answers with pride in his voice: "I planted it myself. My tree. I will care for it and when it's big I will sleep in its shade!"

It is my strong belief that we all, as human beings, need the conscious connection to nature in order to live a full and happy life. Life in general, and in this context mindfulness, is about connections: connection to ourselves, to others, to our environment, to nature, to the universe and beyond. We are all part of a big "whole"; anything we do and say has an effect on something else, which is why it is so important to be mindful in our thoughts, words and actions. I have always been fascinated by the theory of the "butterfly effect", which is part of chaos theory. Chaos Theory is a field of study in mathematics, with applications in several disciplines including meteorology, sociology, physics, engineering, economics, biology, and philosophy. In layman's terms, it basically studies the "knock-on-effect" of a highly sensitive action, such as the flutter of butterfly wings, and the unforeseeable major effects that can be triggered by such "insignificant" actions.

THE OUTDOORS AND HEALTH

To me, personally, mindfulness plays a big part in our physical and mental health. Outdoor experiences have a significant effect on our health, both physically and mentally. I remember when I was growing up the first thing my mother did when we were getting a cold, was wrap us up in warm clothes and take us outside into the fresh air. I can still hear my father saying: "There is nothing better than fresh clean air to cure a flu." I guess my parents were both very old-fashioned as well as progressive in their views of physical health and well-being. It might be a German thing, but since I can remember before applying any prescribed medicines or therapies we would exhaust all the "alternative" routes such as cold leg wraps when we had a fever, teas, honey and home-made rubs for colds and flus and lots and lots of outdoor activities and fresh air. Many of the alternative methods I grew up with and which are probably a bit "German" are based on the work of Sebastian Kneipp (1821-1897), a Bavarian priest who is one of the founders of the naturopathic medicine movement. The methods might sound a bit odd and even cruel to people not familiar with them, but I fondly remember squealing and laughing as we ran around our house and barefoot in the snow in the middle of winter! Don't get me wrong, if there was something a bit more serious than colds and flus, we were brought to a doctor straight away to be checked out. Another sentence I always remember my mother and father telling us, which didn't mean a lot at the time, was: "Fresh air and nature are important for your immune system!"

When we are born, our immune system is not balanced or developed yet. Babies ideally get their first important immunity through the first breast milk, the colostrum, and also through breastfeeding thereafter. Basic vaccinations are usually given throughout the first years of childhood, but they just protect against very specific viruses and illnesses, such as whooping cough, measles, some forms of meningitis etc. Immunity against more common and

105

in most cases less dangerous "bugs" are built up through contact with them throughout our lives. Renz-Polster and Huether suggest that children who grow up on farms or in families that keep pets, in particular dogs, often develop less allergies, as animals store a bacterial decomposition product in their fur, the so-called endotoxins, which keeps the immune system "fit". Plants also contain substances that have a similar effect on our immune system, in other words, anywhere where children get into direct contact with natural environments, they train and develop their immune system.

Another major health benefit of being outdoors is physical movement and exercise. Medical handbooks state: Physical inactivity is the cause or partial cause of half of all occurring illnesses. Regular exercise regulates the metabolism, strengthens the cardiovascular system and stabilises the psyche. It also aids the prevention of cancer and supports general well-being. Science also shows that exercise is beneficial for our minds. Children learn better when they exercise sufficiently. Scientists presume this is due to the dopamine produced in the brain, which helps the establishment of learning experiences and supports self-confidence. Even though we humans unfortunately don't have a natural drive for exercise, as we like to save energy, this is thankfully not the case for children, whose urge to exercise is driven by play. Other health benefits of being outdoors, presented by Renz-Polster, include the following:

- The exposure to the sun, which is important for the production of vitamin D, strengthening of the immune system, and the production of dopamine and other important physical messengers. Of course care has to be taken to protect children's skin against harmful UV exposure.

- The development of our vision: Australian scientists have proof that short-sightedness is not only caused by watching too much television or sitting at a computer, but also by less than two hours of exposure to daylight/sunlight per day.

- "Mens sana in corpore sano" – "A healthy mind in a healthy body". The Romans knew that physical and mental health can't be separated – if the body is healthy this has a positive effect on the mind and vice versa.

The spiritual importance of nature

"Forget not that the earth delights to feel your bare feet and the winds long to play with your hair."

KAHLIL GIBRAN

I believe humans can lead a happy life without religion as such. However, I also strongly believe the human race needs some form of spirituality. I actually think spirituality is not a choice – it's something that we all encounter in some form at some point in our lives, whether we think we are spiritual beings or not. Saying that, I don't mean dramatic apparitions of saints or spirits long gone. To me spirituality is a much more subtle, yet powerful concept. One of the foundations of mindfulness is a "beginner's mind". With a beginner's mind we can see each experience as it really is without preconceived ideas of how we think things should be. We can see things with fresh eyes. In his book, *Last Child in the Woods*, Richard Louv recounts the description Rabbi Martin Levin of Congregation Beth-El gave of "spirituality", which connects it very closely to the concept of a beginner's mind as I understand it:

To be spiritual is to be constantly amazed. To quote the words of Abraham Joshua Heschel, a great teacher of our age, our goal should be to live our life in radical amazement. Heschel would encourage his students to get up in the morning and look at the world in a way that takes nothing for granted. Everything is phenomenal, everything is incredible, never treat life casually. To be spiritual is to be amazed.

To me this is one of the most profound, yet simple, definitions of spirituality. It's probably because it really resonates with me. I am fortunate enough to have a "natural beginner's mind" much of the time; others might call it being "a bit off the wall", as I could come out with any statement such as, "Wow, aren't frogs just fascinating!" or "Can you believe chickens can make one egg a day in their little bodies?" I have caused a raised eyebrow more than once. I am always amazed by things around me. Nature, in particular, has always captured my imagination. Since childhood, I have continued to have my most spiritual experiences in nature. I remember being on holidays in my aunt's house one summer. I was eight or nine years old and sitting on a swing at dusk. The sky was still slightly blue but tinted with pinks and oranges of the lowering sun, silhouettes of buildings and trees were already black. Everything was still apart from the creaking of the swing. A beautiful feeling of being free and safe at the same time came over me. The peace and sheer joy made me physically tingle and laugh out loud. Another treasured memory, again in the summertime, involved one evening after a long spell of hot weather. Very quickly black clouds gathered seemingly out of nowhere, and the heavens opened to release a torrential rain shower. Nothing would have kept me inside. I took off my shoes and socks and danced outside with the warm raindrops which quickly swelled into little streams and big puddles. I could have burst with happiness and excitement, and again it was both a physical and spiritual experience that presented itself out of the blue. I have many more similar memories, and this connection to and amazement of

nature has stayed with me. Anytime I go for a walk in a forest, at a beach or anywhere in the countryside, I stop every so often to feel the nourishing sensation of "being part of creation". Nothing else is important in these moments and even just a few seconds last a long time in my memory.

It is of no surprise to me that there is now scientific focus on and evidence of our spiritual life experiences starting in early childhood. It is supported by a small group of psychologists such as Edward Hoffman, Robert Cole and Abraham Maslow. Hoffman's research suggests that "conventional psychology and its allied disciplines have painted a badly incomplete portrait of childhood, and, by extrapolation, of adulthood as well". Both Hoffman and Cole's findings have evidence, through reports collected from children, that not only are transcendent childhood experiences possible, but that most spiritual childhood experiences seem to happen in nature.

In her powerful article "Playing Outside Nurtures Spirituality in

Children", Traci Pedersen sums up why nature is important in the development of our children's spirituality as well as their physical and mental health.

> Do you remember—when you would spend time in nature as a child—how you would notice the tiniest things? The fuzzy outer layer of a leaf, the intricate pattern on a ladybug's back, the smell of the grass? Do you remember the sense of wonder and awe? The feeling of connection to the earth? Not only is playing in nature good for a child's body and brain, it is good for the soul.

Gretel Van Wieren, assistant professor of religious studies at Michigan State University, along with fellow researcher Stephen Kellert from Yale University, asked themselves the question: "Is it just a myth that children have this deep connection with nature?" They discovered some profound truths. Children who spend a significant amount of time playing outside (five to ten hours per week) feel peaceful, spiritually connected to the earth and believe that they play a role in its protection. Child participants of their study, aged seven to eight, provided information in a variety of ways such as in-depth interviews, drawings, diaries and additional information was gathered through conversations with the parents.

The findings were published in the "Journal of the Study of

Religion, Nature and Culture" and illustrated that children who spend a lot of time outside often experience feelings of peace, awe and a sense of belonging in nature. Researchers commented how some children are even awestruck and humbled by nature's force (i.e. storms, floods) and believe that a higher power created the world. Children who spend plenty of time playing outdoors also have a great appreciation for natural beauty with all its shapes, patterns, symmetry and colours, which supports their curiosity, creativity and imagination.

The researchers also discovered that the parents of children with the strongest spirituality grew up with a strong connection to the outdoors and nature. Parents themselves believed that their own spirituality was enhanced by spending much of their childhood outside. Gretel Van Wieren believes that nature can inspire children through its incredible display and multitude of colours, sights and sounds. Nature is "in a constant state of flux" which greatly supports problem-solving skills. Through its uncertainty, its multi-sensory qualities and "above all, its aliveness" nature gives great opportunities to foster these important skills. Van Wieren adds that through modern life challenges, a harmful distance between humans and nature has been created. Fortunately however, Pedersen says, we can do something about this:

> Let's encourage our children to get outside—to sink their toes in the sand, to study the grass, to feel the wind in their hair—so that the aliveness of nature can infuse their souls with beauty and order and wonder.

ANIMALS (PETS) AND HUMANS:

"What is man without the beasts? If all the beasts were gone, men would die from great loneliness of spirit, for whatever happens to the beast also happens to the man. All things are connected. Whatever befalls the earth befalls the sons of the earth."

CHIEF SEATTLE, LETTER TO PRESIDENT PIERCE, 1855

Since the beginning of time, animals have been evolutionarily very closely interlinked with humans. Apart from the basic and obvious connection of providing food (meat, eggs, milk), clothing (fur, wool, leather), transport (horses, donkeys, elephants, ox), protection and materials for other essential parts of human life (leather, bones, horn etc.), the connection I am talking about in this context is the ancient and unique "partnership" and "friendship" we have formed with animals. The partnership and bond between humanity and horses, for example, dates back to the end of the Ice Age. First signs of horses used as a mount were found at Dereivka in the Ukraine in the Copper Age; this included proof of distance travel, trade and communication indicating a big change in human socialisation. From that time of early equine domestication, the footsteps of humans and horses have been side by side throughout history, which is illustrated in biology, art, music, literature, archaeology and ethnography. Horses have influenced civilization more than we will ever know. From Geronimo to Ghengis Khan, Pegasus to Alexander the Great, Don Quixote to Black Beauty, the horse has influenced the expansion of empires, has been the subject of paintings and poetry, the partner in battle and trade and the first wheels were pulled by "horsepower". Most importantly, in relation to this book, horses are, and have been, a faithful, patient and reliable friend.

As the incredible Dr Temple Grandin, who is on the Autistic Spectrum herself, writes in her and Catherine Johnson's book, *Animals in Translation:*

> I wish more kids could ride horses today. People and animals are supposed to be together. We spent quite a long time evolving together, and we used to be partners. Now people are cut off from animals unless they have a dog or a cat … riding a horse isn't what it looks like: it isn't a person sitting in a saddle telling the horse what to do by yanking on the reins. Real riding is a lot like ballroom dancing or maybe figure skating in pairs. It's a relationship.

It's not just horses that have had a close relationship with humans; there are multiple examples of close bonds and relationships between humans and animals. The most common and probably closest bond seems to be between dogs and humans.

Many years ago, before I had children, I attended a loving-kindness retreat in a beautiful Buddhist retreat centre in the south of Ireland. One of the initial exercises consisted of us imagining the "embodiment of unconditional love" and working with that vision. I stayed in a cottage on-site with three other ladies whom I had never met before. We had a lovely chat after dinner, discussing the experience of the day and meditation practice, especially of what we imagined was an "embodiment of unconditional love". This might sound odd to some, but the answer to this for me was very easy: "It was my beloved dog." I expected them to be surprised, but it turned out that all three women, all happily married with stable family backgrounds, had the same feelings towards their animals. Now let me explain my sentiment a bit better. This by no means meant that I loved my dog more than anybody or anything else, but this was about "unconditional love". Most loving human relationships of any kind, even if we don't think so initially, involve conditional love: I love you because we have the same interests; I love you because I find you attractive; I love you because you care for me and cook me lovely dinners; I love you because you make me feel good. Apart from a parent's love for their children, only very rarely if ever is our love towards others, and unfortunately even towards ourselves, "unconditional".

Pets, in particular dogs, are in a very different category of relationship. They love their humans unconditionally in normal circumstances. Fair enough, they love them even more if there are biscuits or sausages involved, but generally speaking a dog will greet us every evening coming home with a wagging tail and friendly face. They don't judge us for being a little grumpy or impatient. They forgive us our shortcomings and just take us for what we are. I want to make clear at this point that I am referring to "normal" situations where people treat their pets well and don't display abusive behaviours towards them.

My dog Harry has been one of the greatest mindfulness teachers for me. Apart from his non-judging, loving relationship to our family and anybody else he meets for that matter, he also displays incredible compassion and kindness, especially when a family member is sick, unwell or upset. My husband had a severe accident at work some years ago, and I can safely say that our dog was his life saver. He would not leave his side to the extent that he would refuse to sleep anywhere else than by his bedside. For the extremely difficult months and years after the initial accident as I was at work for the majority of the day, Harry was his best friend and companion. Without Harry, my husband's depression following the accident would have overwhelmed him. Of course my husband didn't rely solely on our dog in relation to his mental health and overall well-being, but he played a significant part in his recovery.

Nowadays, dogs in particular are playing a significant part in education and various therapeutic approaches to bridge the widening gap between humanity and nature. Some animals seem to have unique qualities and abilities to connect with humans and often enable communication that wouldn't be as easily achieved without them. There are many examples of their ability to enable communication in children with autism, as animals often display visual ways of non-verbal communication such as wagging tails, body tension, physical movements etc. which frequently seem to open a door and make communication and interaction possible. The term "Pet Therapy" goes back to 1969, when the American psychotherapist Boris M. Levinson discovered by accident that pets could have a profound beneficial impact in therapeutic settings. One day he was visited by a family with their son before their arranged appointment time, and Levinson had his dog Jingles with him in the practice. The boy had always refused any contact and verbal communication with people prior to that day. Jingles greeted the boy enthusiastically, and he was instantly drawn in by the dog, so much so that he asked if the dog was always going to be there in future sessions if he agreed to come back. From that day on Levinson regularly brought his dog to many of his clients and "Pet Therapy" was born.

Animals help us humans both in recognised therapeutic approaches and in the general improvement of life quality. These approaches are now officially defined and referred to as Animal Assisted Therapy (AAT) and Animal Assisted Activity (AAA). Whereas AAT requires specifically trained personnel and animals, AAA typically relies simply on the presence of the animal having a positive effect in various settings such as nursing homes, educational provisions and hospitals etc. Recognised therapies and training include "hippotherapy" and other equine-assisted therapies; assistance dogs for specific conditions such as autism, physical disabilities, blindness and diabetes; dolphin therapy and more. Oftentimes AAT and AAA can overlap, depending on the setting and intervention.

From an educational and parental point of view, I believe that children growing up with animals can support the learning of many life skills and experiences naturally. Children learn to take on responsibilities such as feeding their pets and caring for their well-being, become more independent, treat other creatures with love and kindness, experience unconditional love and regulate their own reactions and behaviours. The benefits are many. In addition, and to put it very simply, pets can be a child's best friend and companion, who will be at their side whenever they need them. They share happy and sad times and are simply there when they might be feeling lonely or misunderstood.

I understand it is not always feasible for families to keep pets, and I don't think that families without pets are necessarily unhappier than people with pets. I do believe though that if at all possible, children benefit greatly from regular contact with animals, not just in their own home. Children should grow up with an awareness that even though they might not live with an animal, they are influenced and supported, even nourished by them on a daily basis, and it is our responsibility as humans to keep that awareness to the forefront in order to include animals in caring for our environment and the world we live in.

INSTILLING CARE, RESPECT AND KINDNESS FOR OUR ENVIRONMENT AND THE WORLD WE LIVE IN

Primarily thanks to the media, children are growing up with a profound sense of threat and fear concerning global environmental issues. I don't want to take away from the dangers and difficult issues the human race is confronted with in relation to our beautiful planet, quite the contrary. I believe though that we need to take a different approach with our children. I have touched on this area briefly before: children are confronted with abstract and frightening information they are unable to put into context, nor are they able to relate to it properly. This causes fear and a sense of helplessness and confusion. There seems to be a large discrepancy between many children's actual experience and enjoyment of their environment on one hand, and the bombardment mainly by the media of upsetting and threatening global issues and occurrences on the other hand.

In order for children to take responsibility and have respect for our planet, they need to get opportunities to connect with it on their level. Global warming, the threat of extinction to species, environmental disasters or the extent of plastic pollution to our oceans are real and frightening issues even for us grown-ups, but they're on much too large a scale for little minds, hearts and heads. Children need an immediate connection to the world that surrounds them, and only then can they be guided towards the bigger issues at a later stage of their lives. We as parents need to be mindful of what our children pick up from the radio, television and internet. Some might think I am a bit over the top, but I won't even expose my children to ad breaks, as even during daytime hours, ads from various charitable foundations, for example, are much too graphic for young children to understand and will only cause fear and confusion, especially when left to watch television on their own.

Getting back to the topic of outdoor experiences, children should be guided towards environmental issues and the importance of treating our world with kindness from the bottom up. There are so many simple activities in which children can get involved to take care of nature and protect our environment as a direct experience. Here are just a few examples of how children can get stuck in:

- You could explain how important bees and other insects are for plants, for food production and for us humans.

- Sow a small patch of wildflowers in the garden or even a pot on the balcony together if you don't have a garden to provide a "home" for insects.

- Build "insect hotels" and find a nice space for it.

- In winter, build bird feeders together and hang them up where you can see the birds feeding.

- Organise a walk to clean up your street, your forest, your village green, a pond or stream. (Wow! That rhymes as my three-year-old would say.)

The possibilities are endless and you can get inspiration from your direct surroundings. Children love getting actively involved and take great pride in their achievements. With this approach they experience the importance of being kind not only to fellow humans, but to animals, plants and everything else in our environment.

A topic children will learn about in school is waste, recycling and re-using, which is a current and very important area. Again this topic should be approached in an age-appropriate manner. Yes, I believe children should know that producing too much rubbish is harmful to our environment, but rather than explaining the global threats at a young age, make them aware of their direct environment. When going for a walk, point out bits of rubbish thrown out into hedges and ditches and explain why this is not a good idea, be it from a cosmetic or pollution angle. Explain that anything made from plastic does not rot (at least not in the next 400 years) and get back to a natural state, and therefore it is important to use as little plastic as possible.

As I said before, I grew up in Germany and environmental issues were addressed both at home and in school from when I was a young child in the late 1970s, early 1980s. This is probably why I am passionate about teaching kids the importance of a responsible approach to environmental issues. We were not allowed to bring anything wrapped into school. Sandwiches had to be kept in a reusable lunchbox and drinks were put in an insulated glass bottle. I can't remember a time when we didn't have to recycle our waste, and if anybody was ever caught "dumping", they were in for severe fines. I remember chatting to people that had visited Germany when I moved to Ireland first, and their main observation was how clean Germany was. I didn't know it any other way, so I found it amusing that cleanliness was the main memory from my home country. This is over twenty years ago and in fairness things have moved on a lot since then, but I was shocked that in a country as stunning as Ireland people would get off scot-free after dumping washing machines, televisions, anything, including the kitchen sink, into a ditch along the road. I clearly remember when I was living with a lovely family on a beautiful farm, being sent with a lighter and a full rubbish bag to the "incinerator" which turned out to be an empty metal barrel. I was physically not able to do the deed and quite honestly was in disbelief and shock. Thankfully things have changed dramatically in the past twenty years in Ireland, and waste prevention, recycling and especially promoting locally grown produce are second to none here.

The key to this issue, like so many others, is early intervention with our children. When routines and rituals as well as certain behaviours are modelled and introduced from a young age, they will become naturally integrated. When going shopping watch out for products that don't have additional plastic or other wrapping, use your own shopping basket or bags. Farmer's markets and farm shops are a great experience for children, and apart from reducing your waste you also support local businesses selling locally grown produce. Be a role model and stay mindful about what you buy and how you recycle your rubbish.

My biggest pet hate used to be our reliance on bottled water when we were living in a rented house. Our tap water was undrinkable unless boiled, so we used quite a lot of plastic bottles, which I was very uncomfortable about, even though we were vigilant in recycling them. The single best investment we made in recent years is the installation of a good water filter, and we haven't bought a plastic water bottle in years. There are so many ways in which we all can make a contribution towards reducing waste. Sometimes all we need is a small idea or impulse to spring into action. If children are made aware from a very young young age about reducing and re-using, it becomes natural to them.

Chapter 11

Mens sana in corpore sano – a healthy mind in a healthy body

In the previous chapter, I touched briefly on the topic of health. I believe that anything in life should be seen and approached with a wholesome and balanced view, and an open mind. To me a mindful way of life includes being mindful of how we fuel and treat our bodies as much as regular mindfulness and meditation exercises. In my definition, a large part of happiness is a healthy body, obviously along with a healthy mind. As someone who has suffered ill health in the past and is suffering from some chronic health issues, I know the effects illness, pain or simply feeling unwell can have on our general well-being and happiness. I know some aspects of health and well-being can be somewhat out of our control, but I also know from my own experience that we can influence our health positively by treating our bodies with love and respect, by "listening" carefully to its needs and feeding it wholesome and nourishing food. There is plenty of research available that proves what we eat and drink, as well as how we exercise, has a big effect not only on our weight (which unfortunately seems to be the most important concern in the media), but on our general physical and mental health and well-being. If we want to lead a happy life it is an utter priority to treat our bodies and consequently our health responsibly.

I am not talking about complicated diets and strenuous exercise routines. I am talking about common sense. I am no doctor, personal trainer, dietician or nutritionist, that's why I will keep this chapter short and just leave it as an impulse for you to keep in mind. Think about what you eat and drink, choose what you think will do you and your body good, and yes, if in moderation that may very well sometimes be a chocolate chip cookie or a slice of pizza! I am a great believer in the 80:20 approach, if there is such a thing. Eighty per cent of the time stick to the healthy (yet nutritious AND delicious) stuff, and then why not once a week have that Indian takeaway if that's what you fancy. As long as you are mindful of what is good for you (for your body AND your mind and soul) and what will have a positive effect for you, go for it! Bring the dog for a walk, enjoy a stroll on the beach, roll around the garden playing ball with the kids. If you enjoy it, run your marathons! To me it's all about balance, which will tilt to one or the other side for all of us sometimes and that's perfectly okay too.

The Madeleine Effect

Food is obviously a necessity for human survival, but it is so much more when we really think about it. Food is pleasure; food connects to family; food is tradition; food is connection to nature and the people who produce it. Food creates and evokes memories, connects people socially and is the key ingredient for celebration. Food expresses love and friendship. We all have our favourite meals and foods that have the ability to transport us straight into our childhood, to a memorable holiday, to a treasured memory of a celebration.

When I close my eyes I can instantly recall the delicious scent of our favourite Sunday dinner: roast chicken in a spice-and-herb marinade with home-made chips. Especially around Christmas time, the scents of cinnamon, star anise and oranges bring back precious memories of Advent in Germany and the bounty of delicious treats in our Christmas markets. I could list countless examples of my personal memories connected to certain tastes, smells and foods. There is actually a name for the effect food has on our minds and memories – it is called the "Madeleine Effect" after a passage in Marcel Proust's 1913 novel, *In Search of Lost Time,* in which he describes the experience of the character, who every time after eating the sweet treats (madeleines) is overcome by a warm and comforting feeling and eventually remembers his aunt who had always given him these treats every time he visited her.

This effect has since been studied by many scientists, and it was discovered that it is actually our sense of smell, which goes hand in hand with our sense of taste, that is responsible for connecting food and emotional memories from the past. The reason for this most probably lies in the structure of our brains, as (in simple terms) our noses transport scents straight into the areas of our brain responsible for our emotions, namely the amygdala and the hippocampus. Also it is often found that olfactory memories go back further into our early childhood than many other memories, as we tend to connect scents and experiences, especially in our early childhood years, as researched by Stockholm University psychologist Maria Larsson.

In recent years this phenomenon has been proven to be very beneficial in therapeutic circumstances when working with senior citizens. Joerg Reuter, author of *Wir haben einfach gekocht* (translated: *We simply cooked*), started an initiative to improve nutrition in nursing homes and collected old recipes and traditions in the process. It transpired that many older people who had become quite withdrawn and quiet suddenly became very animated when the conversation surrounded their food memories. The positive effect didn't stop there but became an all-encompassing "perking up". People who hadn't used their hands much for a while were chopping and peeling while exchanging recipes, memories and stories from their childhood. Food doesn't just nourish our bodies, but our minds, hearts and souls. This is why it is so important to create positive and memorable relationships to food for our children and also for ourselves.

MINDFUL EATING

At this point I'd like to mention the mindfulness practice of "mindful eating". Mindful eating is quite simply paying attention while you are eating, paying attention to what you are eating, where it came from, what it tastes like etc. As mentioned above, food shouldn't just be basic fuel but a wholesome enjoyable experience. Due to different circumstances of everyday life, I often find myself eating without even tasting a bite and later looking at my empty plate wondering where it went. I often eat even though I'm not really hungry, just because it's time for breakfast, lunch or dinner. I often overeat because too many other things are occupying my mind and I don't pay attention to when I'm actually full. Some of you might be able to relate to this.

Many mindfulness courses introduce the concept of mindful eating with the "raisin exercise/meditation" which I have included in the practical part. In this exercise participants are asked to touch, smell and see a raisin with a beginner's mind – meaning to be fully aware of all aspects of the raisin as if you've never seen or tasted one before in your life. This might sound a little strange to some, but most people are amazed by the effects of this exercise. To support a mindful-eating approach, the following questions can be helpful even though they might sound a little too obvious initially:

- Why am I eating? (Am I hungry? Am I stressed? Am I sad? Am I frustrated? Am I just eating because it's "dinner time"? Am I trying to "fill a hole"?)

- What am I eating? (Really look at your food – where did it come from?)

- What does it taste and smell like? What are the textures? (Consciously pay attention to the flavours, smells and textures.)

- Who produced and prepared my food?

- Who am I eating with?

Of course it would be unrealistic and tedious to do this with every bite we eat. But if we can just generally become more aware of our food and eating habits and include some more awareness by asking some of the above questions every so often, it could really improve so many aspects of our lives, such as:

- Our relationship to food and our bodies.
- Our attitude and awareness to food shopping and knowledge of where our food came from.
- A connection to our families and family traditions and passing them on to our children.
- Our general enjoyment of eating.
- An awareness of unhealthy habits.
- An attitude of "slowing down" and taking some "me time" when we're eating.

DEVELOPING HEALTHY HABITS WITH AND FOR OUR CHILDREN

Children are still growing and developing, so if we can agree that nutrition and exercise are important for us "grown-ups" in order to be healthy and well, imagine the impact a wholesome and healthy lifestyle versus a diet full of sugar, processed foods and a lack of exercise will have on a growing child. As I have mentioned before, many children nowadays grow up with too much "screen time", too little exercise, an unhealthy diet and reduced opportunities for outdoor experiences. Rather than setting ourselves up for failure with a radical change in everything, start small. Make fruit and vegetable snacks fun (i.e. create little veg faces or fruit bugs), change white rice to wholegrain rice, use natural sugars such as maple syrup or honey for some of your baking, go for an adventure treasure hunt outside, if you like activities at the weekend seek out trips such as outdoor parks, the beach, pet farms, pick-your-own fruit farms. Every small change will make a difference and if you make it fun and motivating it won't be a struggle.

Children have a natural urge to learn, especially when it is a wholesome and meaningful experience. Many children nowadays don't actually know where their food comes from, and a great way to engage children in healthy eating is involving them in growing their own food. You don't have to have a big garden; food can be

grown on windowsills, balconies and in pots in your home. This experience isn't necessarily just about providing all of your food, which is obviously unrealistic. But even if you just grow some cress, herbs, a tomato plant or some potatoes in a car tyre, children will get an insight into where our food comes from

and learn about the process. Nothing tastes as good as something you have just picked from your own garden or pot, and the caring and nurturing have the additional benefit of providing opportunities to instil responsibility, independence, kindness and a sense of pride and achievement.

Excursions are always an adventure for children. To see first-hand how food is produced is always a motivating way of learning. Many food producers are only too happy to show you around, either as a family or a school class. Farms, bakeries, fruit and vegetable growers etc. often have designated programmes and tours for children to actively get involved in and experience the processes involved in food production. The highlight is usually the tasting of the products, and most children are curious and adventurous to try new things.

Another great way to actively involve our children in a healthy lifestyle is to include them when we are cooking or baking. Unfortunately, there seems to be a trend towards losing many cooking and food preparation skills in recent years due to changes in lifestyle and in the circumstances of modern life. Celebrity chefs, such as Jamie Oliver and Hugh Fearnley-Whittingstall, have picked up on this deficit and thankfully there seems to be an increase of positive initiatives on national and communal levels. Many of these initiatives have started in local communities to counteract this trend and re-introduce families and children to the "art" of cooking and food preparation. There has been an increase in artisan food producers using traditional methods and raising awareness of the origin of our "daily bread". Food fairs and festivals have become more and more popular, and workshops and courses can greatly support families in keeping cooking traditions alive. Children love the experience of cooking, and there are so many opportunities for children to get stuck in.

Let them help with the chopping, mixing and tasting. Let them have their say in planning the meals, starting in the shop or the market. There are many non-cook recipes that children can make independently from a young age once equipment and materials are set out for them. You know your children best – the more independence you can give them, the more pride and a sense of achievement they will get out of the activity. Of course health and safety is a major factor in the kitchen, but with the proper supervision, cooking and baking can become an enjoyable experience for the whole family.

Another important area for creating healthy habits is exercise. I personally don't believe in stringent exercise regimes for young children, unless they are really into a certain sport themselves. Of course children should be engaged in exercise, be introduced to different kinds of sports and learn about being part of a team, but it should be age-appropriate, motivating and fun. I recently observed a training session of a kids' running club, just because the track was right beside a playground we visited. A small group of four or five young boys were training for a relay race, and I was actually quite appalled by what the attending parents thought was acceptable behaviour by the coach who was constantly shouting abuse and criticism at them. I do believe in the necessity and benefits of physical activity though, and again this can be integrated easily into daily routines without making it "a designated time for exercise" i.e. adding another slot to the schedule. There are so many everyday opportunities to integrate exercise naturally and to make it play-based. Depending on where you live, cycle or walk to the shop, school or friends' houses. Take the dog for a walk or go to the local playground to meet up with friends. Encourage ball games, hide-and-seek, egg-and-spoon/pebble races in the park or the back garden.

It's all about education and encouragement in a meaningful and motivating way. It is our responsibility as parents and educators to promote positive, wholesome and healthy habits, and we will be most successful if it's fun and exciting too.

Chapter 12

Touch – essential connection and communication

The first connection a baby has with its mother after birth is through loving touch: through holding, cradling, stroking, kissing and caressing. Skin-to-skin contact is recommended straight after the baby is born and is especially important for premature babies. My first daughter, Julianna, was born by emergency section, and she was taken up to the room straight away. I was devastated. My most vivid and treasured memory of the birth of my second daughter, Jona was the instant skin-to-skin contact we shared. Luckily, the previous week, there had been in-service training in the hospital on the importance of initial contact between mother and child.

I know there is a myriad of parenting books out there, and parenting styles and opinions differ greatly on various topics. Both my girls had terrible colic when they were born, and the endless crying and sleepless nights were challenging to say the least. In despair, I sought "professional" advice and read diverse opinions in books and articles. I quickly realised that the only thing for me was to listen to my instincts rather than to follow regimented routines and methods. I distinctly remember my horror of one approach that recommended leaving the baby to cry and refraining from picking them up and holding them. This was the point when I put all books aside and decided to go with the flow.

I have no doubt that physical touch was our saving grace. This reassuring, loving and calm approach was fundamental in getting us through those challenging times and that includes me being touched by my children. Many years ago, I saw a documentary about an orphanage in Romania. There were many babies in little cots in a large dormitory, and the reporter commented on how quiet the room was. One of the nurses explained that children stop crying after a few weeks because they know nobody will come and pick them up. Their silence denoted resignation. I sobbed and sobbed at the thought of this happening to little babies. It was too heartbreaking to comprehend and even as I am writing this I have tears in my eyes. Young children need physical contact with their parents or guardians.

Our busy, modern lifestyles have resulted in children attending various childcare facilities for much of the time. My experience as a parent and a teacher had led me to believe that this has diminished the necessary levels of intimacy and physical contact between children and parents. It is a well-researched fact that children need touch and physical closeness in order to fully develop mentally, emotionally and even physically.

Myla and Jon Kabat-Zinn's book on mindful parenting, *Everyday Blessings*, presents the following passage on touch, which I wholeheartedly agree with:

> Touch involves being in touch. It can be a unifying experience. We cannot touch without being touched back. It is one way we know we are not alone. Depending on how we are touched, we can feel loved, accepted and valued, or ignored, disrespected, assaulted.
>
> Touch generates awareness and puts us in touch with the world. We touch and are touched through all our senses, seeing, hearing, smelling, tasting, as well as feeling through the skin. Being held with sensitivity grounds us in our bodies

and awakens a sense of connectedness. It awakens us to ourselves and to the other. A child's whole being is honoured when he is touched with awareness, sensitivity, and respect. Learning to be 'in touch' with how you feel while you are young grows out of this experience of feeling safe and cared for. Through holding, hugging, cradling, snuggling, smelling, swinging, rocking, humming, chanting, singing, gazing, parent and child both experience the fullness of being alive.

Touch is essential in building up trust and giving emotional security. It is also an important form of non-verbal communication. The three pro-social emotions – love, gratitude and sympathy – can instantly be communicated through touch. It worries me greatly that many childcare and child-education services have introduced "no-touch" policies. While it is most important to keep our children safe and adhere to strict child-protection guidelines, it is also essential for young children to get appropriate physical feedback, especially when they are in distress. Psychologist Sylvia Clare goes so far as to say that "no-touch" policies are in themselves abusive, as touch is an intrinsic part of emotional literacy and intuitive wisdom, a kind of self-knowledge that shapes our ability to read situations and assess how to deal with them appropriately. The experiences children receive throughout their life shape the way their brains develop. Children who do not receive sufficient appropriate touch are unable to form important neural connections. This leads to them becoming desensitised. Such children, notes Clare, are likely to develop into people who lack empathy, emotional warmth and the basic ability to engage in normal human/adult relationships. They are also more vulnerable to contact involving inappropriate touching because they lack positive touching experiences.

I have worked with young children with autism between the ages of three and eight for most of my teaching career. Many present with impaired sensory processing, which can frequently result in inappropriate physical behaviours such as slapping, pushing, kicking or pinching. These behaviours occur without ill intentions or even any intention at all and are often triggered by sensory overload or even under-stimulation. The resulting stress, anxiety and even physical pain explain why children can have a meltdown. Children with autism can sometimes appear as if they do not want to be touched, but this is the perfect example for the consideration of personal preferences and needs. The formidable Dr Temple Grandin gave the following description of how she used to perceive touch as a child:

> As a child, I craved to feel the comfort of being held, but I would pull away when people hugged me. When hugged, an overwhelming tidal wave of sensation flowed through me. At times, I preferred such intense stimulation to the point of pain, rather than accept ordinary hugs. On the Ayres Checklist for Tactile Defensiveness (1979), I had 9 out of 15 symptoms by age 10 years. Whenever anyone touched me, I stiffened, flinched, and pulled away. This approach-avoidance characteristic endured for years during my childhood.

Grandin subsequently developed a "squeeze machine" to help her overcome her over-sensitivity to touch. It would not only be counterproductive if we were forced to adhere to a "no-touch" policy in the environment I teach in, I am convinced it would also have devastating and detrimental effects on our teaching and on the children themselves. It is essential our students become aware of their own preferences and learn about appropriate and positive touch.

Referring to the importance of touch and "no-touch" policies, Michael Ungar, a professor of social work and author of *The We Generation: Raising Socially Responsible Kids,* says: "It's unfortunate that we're moving away from such things … In our efforts to keep kids safe — implementing no-touch policies in schools, for example — we risk imposing sterility in relationships. How are kids going to learn to distinguish good and bad touch if they never experience it outside of home?" Children need language to talk about it; this is what will keep them safe. It is our responsibility as parents and educators to talk openly about appropriate and inappropriate behaviours in order to give our children the tools to express themselves when they feel they have been taken advantage of or made to feel uncomfortable by somebody else.

Touch is essential for our physical health and well-being. Tiffany Field, director of the Touch Research Institute at the University of Miami School of Medicine, says, "Physical contact is important across the lifespan, positive touch stimulates pressure receptors under the skin, lowering the heart rate, slowing the breath, decreasing stress hormones and boosting the immune system. In other words, touch helps bodies stay healthy." Science has shown that positive touch lowers depression and anxiety. Touch can be seen as a kind of shorthand, a powerful way to communicate affection, care and concern for your child.

There have been multiple disturbing experiments throughout the centuries to explore whether children need language and/or physical touch. One was famously conducted by the German King Frederick II (1194–1250) who removed infants from their mothers and placed them into the care of nurses, who were instructed to neither speak to them nor touch them. To the king's great dismay, his experiment was cut short because the babies died! Anna Freud, daughter of Sigmund Freud, was working with children after the Second World War. She discovered that children who were sent away to foster homes in the country to avoid the blitz were much more traumatised than children who stayed in London with their parents and experienced the bombing. This really showed Ungar's point that children can become far more resilient to potentially traumatising events when they have a strong attachment and are physically close to someone they trust.

When we meet somebody, touch is the first part of a conversation and sets the tone or creates a vibe. Personally, I like affirming straight physical feedback: a firm handshake, a tight hug or a pat on the arm. Everybody is different and we all have our unique preferences. I have some friends who can't bear touchy-feely behaviour as they call it. Others will comfortably chat with their arm around somebody's shoulders. Cultural background is a very important factor, as the etiquette on touch varies greatly throughout the world. What is considered normal and friendly in one country could be mortally offensive in another. In our society of ever-growing diversity this is something we have to be sensitive of.

Positive touch is a non-verbal form of communication and teaches children to read and understand social and emotional cues. Touch is a vital factor in the development of attachment between parents and their children. It's the physical reinforcement to show that we are present, we are there for them. Showing positive touch within our families is how children experience and learn about appropriate touch: what is pleasant and what isn't comfortable. It also teaches them about how relationships work: about boundaries, communicating your feelings and emotions, expressing your needs and responding to someone else's.

An important factor in how much or what kind of physical contact children need is their temperament. Some children are naturally shy and timid and might be more comfortable to be physically close to Mum or Dad. Other kids might be more active and independent and just "check in" for a brief high five. Both children are connecting with their secure base in their own way. This could, amongst other things, have to do with differences in sensory processing or personality and temperament. Some children like sitting on their parents' laps and enjoy gentle caresses and hugs, others love rough physical play bouncing together on the trampoline or tumbling on top of you playing soccer.

My older daughter Julianna has ASD (autism spectrum disorder) and she struggles with sensory issues and body awareness. She is often unaware of her physical strength, and what she perceives as giving a hug, for example, my younger daughter, Jona, might misinterpret as rough wrestling or even a painful attack. This often causes misunderstandings. For us it has been essential to teach both girls about touch: what is pleasant, what isn't, what is acceptable for others and what isn't. Julianna's sensory processing difficulties often make these judgements difficult for her and as touch is such a big part of making social connections, learning about appropriate touch is very important. Touch can only be taught by practical examples rather than theory, especially in our situation. One example is how we explained tickling to her with the phrase "butterfly fingers". This evocation of a gentle flutter was necessary, as her perception of tickling used to be more along the lines of innocent but forceful poking. Touch is also the only thing that will relax Julianna. Her body is quite tense a lot of the day due to her condition and she will actually ask to have her back or feet rubbed in the evening. I can feel her muscles relax instantly, even if it is just for a few minutes. Her favourite is "baking pizza" – an activity you can find in the practical part.

Children's need or desire for touch is also greatly influenced by their age, and while younger children tend to want a lot of physical contact with their parents, an older child or adolescent might start to be a little more embarrassed or self-conscious if you take his/her hand in public. Teenagers might even refuse physical contact from their parents altogether, especially in plain view of their peers, and it's obviously important to respect their personal space, even if it might be difficult for us parents. It's always a good idea to follow your child's lead. Keep up routines like bedtime tuck-ins, goodnight kisses or hugs when leaving them to school. As children get older, find new ways to show your affection if hugs and kisses get "too embarrassing" – a goodbye/hello routine, doing your daughter's hair or high-fives after a sports event can connect you with your teenager. Someday your grown-up child might surprise you with getting back to the hugs and kisses, especially when physical affection was a natural part of their early childhood and upbringing.

Unfortunately, in many homes, time and opportunities to foster intimate and physical relationships have become scarce: parents have a lot more work to do when they come home from mostly full-time jobs, and apart from a bedtime story and a goodnight kiss it's often only the weekends that provide more time for family. Consciously setting special time aside for the whole family to reconnect and nourish body and soul as a unit is essential. If we are mindful of the importance of touch, especially for our children, we have the opportunity to keep that physical bond even through small gestures throughout the day. A hug and kiss dropping them off at the day-care centre or school, the same picking them up, a caress on the cheek when talking to them, holding hands for a little while when going for a walk, a little squeeze on the shoulder when just passing during homework etc. This feedback only takes a split second, but the impact on our children's well-being and the bond between parent and child is significant.

THE IMPORTANCE OF A MULTI-SENSORY APPROACH

Our senses are basically the bridges that connect our brain to our body as well as to the world around us, and they are essential for our protection and orientation. We rely on the information sent by our senses, and none of them can be seen in isolation. All of our experiences are multi-sensory, and we often take this interaction and integration for granted as it happens automatically. When we eat, we usually see, smell, taste and touch the food. When children play, they see their toys, touch them and hear the noises of play. When we are outdoors, we feel our feet touching the ground and the wind on our faces, smell the nature around us, see the sights and hear the birds or the traffic. No matter what we do, our senses are always there to support and make sense of experiences, to make them "whole". When we are confronted with a situation where one or more of our senses are compromised for whatever reason, we become instantly unbalanced, at least for a short moment until our other senses try to piece together the experience for us. We can create these situations artificially: when we are blindfolded, for example. External factors or injury/illness can affect the functioning of one or more of our senses. For most of us, it is only in these situations that we realise how important our senses are for us to, pardon the pun, make sense of our experiences and the world around us. For some of us, due to various circumstances or disabilities, the integration of all the senses can be impaired, and it is all the more important to train, exercise and get exposure through the functioning senses with a multi-sensory approach to life.

We all know about human beings having five senses, but there are actually seven senses. Apart from the external senses that pick up sensory information from the environment – touch, sound, sight, smell and taste – there are two internal senses: the sense of movement and the sense of body awareness. These give you information about your body position and movement in relation to gravity. The seven senses aren't really individual information channels. Everything we experience actually affects more than just one sense, and all sensory input is processed together in the brain in many of the same neurological structures. For example, if you spin around in one place with your eyes open, you will pick up sensory information about body posture, movement, your feet touching the ground, different sights, sounds around you, the wind in your face etc. Life is a multi-sensory experience!

Research shows that a multi-sensory approach is essential for children's learning and development. The involvement of all senses makes teaching and learning a holistic process; topics are "experienced" rather than just read about or taught. A multi-sensory, hands-on approach both helps children to "make sense" of things and concentrate much more easily but from a different angle. It also helps to develop the senses.

For teaching more formal mindfulness meditation exercises to children, I believe a multi-sensory approach is very important. When beginning mindfulness meditation, even adults often find it quite difficult and abstract to "just be", to "sit still", to "hold different parts of your body in awareness" or to be aware of "whatever arises". Children don't have the same body awareness as adults, who at the best of times struggle with REAL body awareness. This is one of the reasons mindfulness meditation is so beneficial: to reconnect body and mind. Verbal instruction alone, without a visual clue or the involvement of other senses, is often too abstract and difficult to follow for children.

The involvement of all senses will help children to focus, to be aware of experiences and their own bodies. Activities, games and stories using sensory materials, visual aids as well as sensory input from their parents or another adult will, in my view, prepare and help children to concentrate and sit for the more formal meditation exercises. Simple stories and visual cues will also help to explain mindfulness and give an understanding of why we practise mindfulness meditation. This approach will also help to deepen relationships, build trust and, last but not least, be fun!

Chapter 13

The lost art of gratitude

"It's not happy people who are thankful; it's thankful people who are happy."

UNKNOWN

Gratitude: The quality of being thankful; readiness to show appreciation for and to return kindness.

OXFORD DICTIONARY DEFINITION

I remember listening to one of Thich Nhat Hanh's Dharma Talks that touched on the topic of gratitude. Apart from him being a wise and very well-spoken man, he has a great sense of humour and an amazing ability to put the sometimes abstract spiritual language into a very clear and simple context. The example he gave has stayed with me and is one of my most profound reminders for being grateful. He spoke about the experience of having a very bad toothache: how painful, uncomfortable and debilitating it is. At the time we might feel very sorry for ourselves and would do anything to stop this pain and suffering. Then, after some treatment or medication, the toothache is gone and we carry on as if nothing happened. Why aren't we grateful for the absence of the toothache? It gave us so much suffering, but once it's gone that's all forgotten! I have never heard a truer or more profound explanation of paying attention and being grateful for our blessings, and ever since I am frequently thankful for NOT having a toothache, NOT having a bad cold, NOT having to worry about my job or NOT having to worry about being evicted from our house. The list is endless and the concept can be applied to anything at all. Of course I am thankful for receiving blessings as well, but this talk will forever be my reminder of how lucky I am and how many things are already in my life to give thanks for.

I believe we all have a "relativity mechanism", and maybe that's the reason why our perception of our own reality and the appreciation for our blessings fluctuate a lot depending on circumstances. I will give you the following personal example to explain what I mean by this, which is probably similar to Thich Nhat Hanh's Dharma Talk example: When I was 19 I was very ill for a few months. It all started with desperate pains, a high fever and my inability to walk. I had already had similar symptoms a few years previously when a benign tumour was detected in my psoas muscle and was successfully treated with medication. This time it seemed more serious. I had to have multiple surgeries, and I was very unwell for a few months, spending most of this time in hospital. I lost a lot of weight very quickly and had no energy whatsoever. It must have been very worrying not just for me but also for my parents. I found out later that my dad had vowed to go on a pilgrimage if I recovered; he kept this promise a few months later. I also made a promise, to myself and God, that if I got through it and came out the other side cured, I would never again in my life complain about typical female concerns like losing weight, not being pretty enough or having crooked teeth, i.e. superficial vanities. As long as I was healthy everything else would be irrelevant. A few months passed, I slowly gained strength and after about a year I had fully recovered. And guess what happened as time passed – I ignored my promise and fell back into old habits and patterns again. Bear in mind, I've been lucky never to have had serious issues about my looks; I've never been a vain person. What I want to illustrate with this example is how much we appreciate certain things seems to depend a lot on our circumstances and frame of mind at the time.

A few weeks ago there was a very tragic incident in a nearby community when a baby lost its life. I was shaken to the core for a few days even though I didn't know the family personally, and again I was ripped out of my bubble for a while, clutching my children close in eternal gratitude every night and counting my blessings. In general, I would class myself as an appreciative person but we all fall into the trap of taking things for granted, and sometimes it takes an external impulse to pull us back into reality and see what's in front of our nose.

I vividly remember one Christmas when I was about thirteen years of age. There was no such thing as writing letters to Santa Claus, partly because we didn't know Santa Claus but the "Christkind", but mainly because presents were a surprise and also an uncertainty, at least in children's minds. I am sure children then, as they do now, wished for gifts, mostly in secret, sending up little hopeful messages into the sky at bedtime, but that's what they were – hopeful wishes. Christmas was magical and a big part of that magic was this uncertainty, the hope, the excitement, even the little bit of fear of not receiving any gifts. After our Christmas dinner, we were ushered out of the sitting room to give the "Christkind" a chance to bring the presents. I was obviously beyond the belief in the "Christkind", but even the knowledge we were getting gifts from our parents was very exciting, and as I am the oldest of three, there were still two "believers" in the house. Upon hearing the "Christkind's" bell we returned to the sitting room where the gifts had been placed under the Christmas tree. Mine was on a chair, and because of its size it was covered with a cloth rather than wrapped with paper. I uncovered the large rectangular shape to discover my mum's stereo, the one she always used for her dancing classes. Now, at this point I am expecting you to take pity on my thirteen-year-old self – a second-hand stereo! But guess what – I was so thrilled with my gift, especially when Mum switched it on to reveal my first CD: the soundtrack to *Dirty Dancing*. I could not have been happier. I felt all grown up and valued as a teenager. I was really grateful, which to me equals being very happy.

I want to emphasise that I am not wagging any fingers or patronising parents. But here's what strikes me more and more today: even though most children get so much more nowadays, they don't in my experience seem proportionally happier. We have all heard and said phrases such as: "No matter what I give him, he's never happy", "The more she gets, the more she wants", "Children take all they have and get for granted". The question we need to ask ourselves is simply: "Why?"

One major factor of course is the change in our lifestyle. When I was growing up, foreign holidays, meals in restaurants, weekends away, playdates and children's activity centres were unheard of for rural middle-class families. We were used to a more frugal life, and treats consisted of small pieces of chocolate, some jelly bears and maybe an ice-cream cone every so often in the summer. The thing about these treats was this: they were TREATS! Something we waited for and looked forward to in anticipation, excitement and sometimes we even had to work for them. Times have changed, and that's okay! There is no point in us wanting our children to lead the same frugal life in a different society. What we need to do though is teach our children the gift of gratitude. Some may say, "Yes, of course we do. It's all about children having good manners and saying 'Thank you' when they receive a present, treat or favour." I completely agree, but in my opinion there is a much more important reason for teaching children to be thankful, and that is, plain and simple, their own happiness! If children get everything they ask for and more, they will have unrealistic expectations for the rest of their lives. There will be an unpleasant wake-up call at some stage that unfortunately things don't come as easily as this all the time. This might happen during a later stage in childhood if the family experiences harder times, or it could happen whenever they start standing on their own feet later on in life. The other problem with "treats on tap" is the habit of taking things for granted, which usually results in not appreciating them and seeing them as an everyday occurrence. When we give treats to our children our intention is usually to make them happy, isn't it? – I know, from my own experience, sometimes they are downright bribes, but let's just say that's the exception!

So, how can we do this? How can we teach gratitude to our children? There are different opportunities to teach gratitude that we can naturally incorporate into our daily lives:

1. **Limit choices and frequency of treats.**
   Do you know the feeling of reading a large menu in a restaurant, struggling to make a choice, and once it's made doubting your choice and thinking you should have picked something else? For me that often affects my enjoyment of the meal. Even as an adult, I struggle with too many choices. Especially for young children, too many choices can not only be overwhelming but will also give them a sense of "We can have anything we want!" This will dilute the meaning of a treat and make it less special to the child. If children take treats for granted, then treats are not treats anymore, which in turn will affect their appreciation and gratitude

for receiving them. It is often a good idea to keep treats a surprise – if they are not expected, the excitement and feeling of gratitude and happiness will be enhanced greatly.

2. **Make your children aware of children who aren't as fortunate as them.**

   You, as the parent, will be the judge of a suitable example for your children. Keep it simple for very young children and maybe show them a picture or picture book of a child who owns only one toy, for example. Older children will be able to learn more about living conditions around the world. It doesn't necessarily have to introduce them to very traumatic examples such as war or extreme starvation, but from my experience children are very interested in other cultures and how children live in other countries. From children living in nomadic families in Mongolia to children living in tribal villages in a South American rainforest or African bush, these examples will clearly illustrate to children the extent of our wealth and comfort. It might also show them that most of these children might lead a very simple yet happy and more grounded life than our children in modern Western society.

3. **Encourage children to be charitable.**

   Following on from teaching an awareness that many other children don't have as much as they do, we can encourage our children to donate to a worthy cause or even just give a helping hand. Clear out the toy box every so often and let the children make a choice in what could be given to a charity or even to children they personally know. There are many ways in which awareness can be created that "giving" can be more joyful than receiving. On a daily basis, this can be done simply by encouraging children to be kind to others, be helpful if you can and share with friends and family even in the smallest way.

4. **Keep a gratitude journal.**

   This can be done daily or at the end of every week. Again, it can be adapted depending on the child's age and ability. Young children can stick on pictures of activities or treats that they particularly liked and have a chat about why they liked them so much. Older children could maybe pick three things they are grateful for or particularly enjoyed every evening and either write them into a journal or make a drawing or painting. This will not only bring to their minds what they are grateful for, but it will also conclude their day in a positive way.

5. **Learn to say "no".**
We all want our children to be happy and fulfil their needs and wishes, but children need to learn that there are boundaries and limits in order to have realistic expectations for the future. The example we give as parents teaches our children what to expect, what is acceptable and what is not. This sometimes means that we need to say "no" and stick to it. We should of course be sensitive and fair even in saying "no". Explain your reasons: "You have had your treat already today", "We can't afford to buy this toy; it's too expensive" or "Tom can come and play another time when we are not as busy". Being consistent and fair will help your child accept rules and understand certain decisions.

6. **Let children earn a treat – teach them the value of money.**
I recently brought my five-year-old daughter shopping. She spotted a toy that she really liked and proceeded to tell me that she was buying it. I looked at her and asked her where she had the money to pay for it. She answered that I had the money, to which I replied that I only had money for our groceries and that she could save up her piggy bank money to buy toys. Now this could have gone either way as many of you can imagine, but even to my surprise she thought about it for a minute, said okay and moved on. I believe that children should know that "money doesn't grow on trees" (Oh, how I hated this expression when I was a child), and that we as parents work hard to keep the boat afloat. Giving children age-appropriate chores to earn a reward is a valuable lesson, and it instils a real sense of appreciation of "I earned this". It also prepares children very slowly and gently for "the real world". There won't be free handouts when they stand on their own two feet in the future, and they won't expect it either.

7. **Show/teach your children where food comes from, preferably wholesome natural foods.**
Even if it's just a small container, plant a small garden and involve the children in caring for the plants. Encourage them to watch the plants grow and then harvest and eat the produce. Children love to get involved and are fascinated by

watching seeds grow into vegetables. If possible, keep some chickens and let the kids help to care for them and collect and use the eggs. Visit a farm or small artisan food producers that make their own cheeses, breads, preserves etc. There are many places around that actually offer workshops and open days to involve children and educate them. Children will appreciate food much more if they know how much work, care and love goes into the production.

8. **Use a reward chart.**
   Some children might find it too difficult or abstract to wait or work for a treat/reward. It often helps to use a reward chart to help your child understand. Start small and rather than using a weekly chart, use a chart for an hour or two. Earn stickers for good behaviour, small acts of kindness, being helpful, finishing homework, brushing teeth and doing a small chore. You know your child best; just tailor the chart to your child's need and ability.

9. **Lead by example.**
   Children learn a lot from us parents and the example we give. Be mindful of your own words and actions. Show appreciation for small things, especially coming from our children. Make much of every picture they paint, every kind gesture they make and every task well done. As parents, we can only teach authentic gratitude if we show genuine gratitude ourselves.

It is important for children to learn to be grateful for things that can't be bought for money. I actually believe that most children intrinsically crave the blessings that aren't materialistic. I love the following story, published by Dan Asmussen, and I think it really illustrates that children still have a natural connection and desire for the "simple things in life" beneath it all.

One day a very wealthy father took his son on a trip to the country for the sole purpose of showing his son how it was to be poor. They spent a few days and nights on the farm of what would be considered a very poor family. After their return, the father asked his son how he liked the trip.
'It was great, Dad,' the son replied.
   'Did you see how poor people can be?' the father asked.
   'Oh, yeah,' said the son.

'So, what did you learn from the trip?' asked the father.

The son answered, 'I saw that we have one dog and they had four. We have a pool that reaches to the middle of our garden, and they have a creek that has no end. We have imported lanterns in our garden, and they have the stars at night. Our patio reaches to the front yard, and they have the whole horizon. We have a small piece of land to live on, and they have fields that go beyond our sight. We have servants who serve us, but they serve others. We buy our food, but they grow theirs. We have walls around our property to protect us; they have friends to protect them.'

The boy's father was speechless.

Then his son added, 'It showed me just how poor we really are.'

Too many times we forget what we have and concentrate on what we don't have. What is one person's worthless object is another's prize possession. It is all based on one's perspective. Sometimes it takes the perspective of a child to remind us what's important.

Discipline versus punishment

We as parents and educators frequently find ourselves in situations where disciplinary intervention is needed, either because of safety issues or unacceptable behavioural occurrences. I know that I often react to a situation in ways that I regret and even judge myself for a second later. It could be that I don't pay attention to what my child is saying, it could be impatiently yelling when after the fifth reminder my daughter still hasn't tidied away her toys, it could be using one of the dreaded phrases of my own childhood like "Because I said so!" or "Oh I hope Santa isn't watching!" I swore pre-parenthood I was NEVER going to utter those sentences. One of my favourites (not!) is loudly shouting, "Will you be quiet now?" Talk about mixed messages! Much of the time this happens when I feel particularly helpless, stressed or scared, when I am tired or unhappy myself and when I am not being mindful.

It is possible, however, to discipline our children without using this term as a synonym for punishment. The actual origin for discipline comes from the Latin word *disciplina,* which means instruction, teaching or knowledge, not punish or punishment. In their book, *No-Drama Discipline,* Daniel Siegel and Tina Payne Bryson say: "You really can discipline in a way that's full of respect and nurturing, but that also maintains clear and consistent boundaries. In other words, you can do better."

We often react to our children on autopilot when they misbehave, and we can find ourselves behaving just as "bad" as our children. I have often caught myself in the middle of a "squabble" doing exactly what I was trying to stop my children from doing, i.e. shouting, not listening, being bossy or not using nice language or tone of voice. Siegel and Payne Bryson encourage us to ask the following three questions before we respond to "misbehaviour":

1. Why did my child act this way?

2. What lesson do I want to teach in this moment?

3. How can I best teach this lesson?

The most important reason we should ask these three questions is because it creates a pause before a reaction. It's a pause to become mindful of the situation. We can assess what and why it is actually happening, and this pause enables us to respond rather than react. These questions will help us to deal with our children in a more meaningful and constructive manner when they display challenging behaviours.

Sometimes there are valid reasons why our children are acting out rather than just being "naughty", especially when children are challenged in their sensory integration processing, are coming down with sickness or are at a certain developmental stage where they haven't yet acquired the appropriate skill such as patience, for example. Explain why certain behaviours are unacceptable, give constructive examples of how some challenging behaviours make others feel. Teach better age-appropriate strategies: "I don't like you kicking my leg when you want my attention, it hurts me. How about putting your hand on my arm and saying: 'Mum, I really need your attention please.'" Alter the environment if needed to make things easier if children struggle with sensory issues (i.e. autism). There are some more ideas around "making things easier" in the following chapter about simplifying our children's lives.

There is no "one-for-all approach" – this simple truth is one of the most invaluable and liberating things I have learned during my teaching career. Every child is different! What might work for one child could have the complete opposite effect on another. Parents and educators know "their" children best and can judge how to provide important guidance and boundaries. What is at the core of discipline is the process of teaching a child the difference between acceptable and unacceptable behaviours. It is about the development of self-control and a moral compass. In short, it is about helping children to grow up into kind, compassionate and responsible adults.

Children need boundaries to help them navigate their lives. Boundaries are nothing other than "guidelines" – literally guiding us and helping us make positive connections. These boundaries don't have to be taught through punishment, but through a mindful connection to our children's stage of development and their personal needs and situation. A key aspect to discipline is the awareness of our own state of mind when we are confronted with a challenging parenting situation. When we become more present and realise we are reacting in a certain way because we are stressed or worried, for example, it will help us greatly to adjust our reaction and become more aware of what is actually happening.

"UPSTAIRS TANTRUMS" VERSUS "DOWNSTAIRS TANTRUMS"

The dreaded tantrum – the behaviour that turns our cherished, sweet little munchkins into unrecognisable, kicking, screaming aliens, and us into sweating, helpless wrecks who feel like we have just lost our parenting license. What to do? We need to look at the causes for these behaviours to understand how we can effectively and calmly manage them or even prevent them if at all possible. A common reason for misbehaviour or challenging behaviours are negative emotions, stress or anxiety, but there can be additional factors that might not be so obvious initially. These can manifest in tantrums and melt-downs that can be sometimes difficult for parents and educators to handle, especially in challenging locations, such as the shopping centre, at the airport, at a function or in a friend's house.

Part of my training, specifically in relation to autism, was learning some key strategies when dealing with challenging behaviours, and I believe that these core strategies are as valid and helpful for any child in distress. First of all, it is important that we stay as calm as possible in order to assess the situation with a level head (see the three questions above). In order to deal with challenging behaviours appropriately we need to know why they occurred. Dan Siegel describes two types of tantrums: an "upstairs tantrum" and a "downstairs tantrum". In relation to brain functioning, Siegel uses the metaphor of "upstairs and downstairs brain" – the downstairs brain is mostly developed even at birth, while the upstairs brain is still immature and stays "under construction"; it's a work in progress until we are in our mid-twenties. This means that our children's brains aren't fully integrated yet, and they might sometimes find it difficult to make good decisions, show empathy and self-understanding and control emotional reactions.

In relation to challenging behaviours this means that there are two types of challenging behaviours or tantrums. The upstairs tantrums means that the child is engaging the upstairs brain and is using their behaviour to achieve something like getting a treat or a certain toy. They are in control of their behaviour and could stop it instantly, as they are using it as a deliberate strategy. Very young children don't have the capacity to have these types of tantrums, which is helpful to know. In this instance parents and educators should set clear boundaries. In Siegel's words: "Never negotiate with a terrorist!" Calmly explain appropriate and inappropriate behaviour and "stick to your guns". It is important to give clear consequences and follow through with them. As mentioned above, they are clear guidelines for your child to learn about appropriate and inappropriate behaviours. If you are consistent, children learn that their strategy is ineffective and will stop using it.

A "downstairs tantrum" is a very different kettle of fish, as the child is not in control of their actions anymore. They could be emotionally or sensorily overwhelmed, unable to access their upstairs brain. Maybe they are in pain, maybe they are in a crowded place which overwhelms them, maybe they are terrified of something or maybe they are missing their mum and are emotionally overwhelmed. In this situation a very different parental/educator's approach is needed. When we are confronted with a stressful situation like this, we tend to get anxious ourselves and start talking at the child in our desperate attempts to calm the child down. This actually has the opposite effect, as it bombards the child with more stimulation during a time when their ability to take in any verbal instruction is very limited. The main methodology we learned in our training was to try and stay as calm as possible and reduce spoken language. We

149

do not want to teach a lesson in this moment. We want to help the child to calm down and access their upstairs brain again. Use short, comforting, reassuring phrases, such as, "It's okay", "Don't worry" and "I'm here". Give calm and compassionate physical feedback: hold the child or stroke their hand or head. If possible, remove them from the situation they can't cope with or remove the trigger for the behaviour (i.e. a loud radio, barking dog).

Chapter 14

Simplifying our children's lives

I believe that most children in our modern Western society are overwhelmed by "too much" while at the same time they are "not getting enough". Too many choices, too many toys, too much technology, too many sensory influences, too many treats, too much pressure, too many activities and too much "stuff". This stands in stark contrast to not enough quiet time, not enough outdoor experiences, not enough structure, not enough quality family time, not enough time to just be a child, not enough opportunities for free, unstructured play. You may think this is contradictory. On one hand there should be more structure, rules and routines; on the other hand children should become independent and have more time for free play or to just be a child. I believe that children need a foundation of predictable structures in order to feel safe and to grow up from a stable base.

The quote from the Dalai Lama at the very beginning of this book illustrates succinctly what I wish for my children: "Give the ones you love wings to fly, roots to come back and reasons to stay." In his book, *Into the Magic Shop*, Dr James Doty, a neuroscientist and brain surgeon, writes: "Children, and adults as well, perform best when there is consistency and dependability. The brain craves them both … Teenagers crave freedom, but only if they are standing on a base that is stable and secure."

Before children are able to be independent and have "wings to fly" they need our help and guidance in order to find their place in the world. For me, that means providing children with a stable and predictable environment involving routines and rules with foreseeable outcomes. Of course there needs to be room for flexibility – we all know life doesn't come with a manual and compass – but if we try our best to help build a framework, some "roots" for our children to grow, they will be able to fly in the future and even weather life's storms along the way.

The TEACCH Approach

I have been teaching young children with autism for the past seventeen years, and I have been fortunate enough to do a lot of training throughout these years. We use an eclectic and open approach in the school I teach in, and we are always open to different interventions and suggestions regarding the individual child and their needs, well-being and learning style. Our overall classroom methodology for children with ASD (Autism Spectrum Disorder) is based on the TEACCH Approach (Treatment and Education of Autistic and Communication related Handicapped Children). This approach was devised in the late 1960s in the Department of Psychiatry at the University of North Carolina. A fundamental part of the TEACCH programme is based on a structured learning environment: classrooms are clearly divided into areas that all serve a different purpose wherever possible i.e. work station, art table, reading corner, free play area, group table etc. It is also important to keep the room tidy and uncluttered in order to keep visual distractions to a minimum. Routines and rituals are introduced to provide structure to daily activities, and tasks are set up in a way that promotes independence, communication and social interactions. Speech is reduced and simplified in order to make communication clear and easy to understand, but also not to flood children with a lot of language they possibly don't understand and which could cause stress and discomfort. Visual aids, such as pictures, arrows, photos and signs, are used to make the environment even more "understandable" and to reduce the need for too much speech. This is only a very short and simplistic description of the intervention, but it touches on the main components which are then tailored to the individual child and their strengths and needs.

I remember doing several TEACCH trainings many years ago and thinking: "Why should this only be a specific approach to teach children with autism?" Everything makes complete sense for teaching any young child of any ability. The structure makes it easy for children to orientate in their environment, and uncluttered rooms prevent unnecessary distractions and possible disruptions. Students are encouraged to work independently, but they are also taught and encouraged to communicate and interact with their peers and teachers. When I became a parent and had more contact with other parents and children as a result, it struck me more and more that elements of the approach I had been working with for years have their place in any home and children's bedroom. In their book, *Simplicity Parenting*, Kim John Payne and Lisa M. Ross put it to the point when they say:

> *"Too much stuff leads to too little time and too little depth in the way kids see and explore their worlds."*

Every Christmas I am both shocked and amused by the sheer craziness of present-mania. Children rip open countless presents only to end up crying, overwhelmed or in many cases playing with the empty boxes and wrapping accessories. I am not being judgemental because I know how helpless many parents feel by the well-meaning annual bombardment of gifts by grandparents, aunts and uncles, friends and neighbours. Their intention of making a child happy often turns out the opposite. I do believe that we as parents have to take ownership and draw lines for the benefit of our children. We have all witnessed that "too much" is just that. We need to take the lead and talk to family members about what we feel is acceptable and what is not. This should of course not be a cause for confrontation, but it is important for others to respect our wishes and decisions for the benefit of our children. In our family, we have come to the agreement that for birthdays and Christmas family members either ask what the children need or offer to put some money towards a bigger present that might be wanted at the time (i.e. bike, tricycle or music lessons). Not only does this reduce the amount of presents, but it also helps the family to be able to afford some presents that might otherwise be too expensive.

IDEAS TO SIMPLIFY CHILDREN'S LIVES

What can parents do to simplify our children's environment and lives? The following suggestions are just pointers and ideas. Every parent knows their children best and should decide what would make things easier for them:

1. Keep your child's room as uncluttered as possible. Include them in the process of what they would like to keep in it and what they can do without.

2. Rotate toys and books. Children usually have too many toys around and often find it difficult to play and choose. Sort out half of them, store them away and after a few weeks swap them. Children sometimes don't even remember what they have, and it's like a mini Christmas when toys are swapped.

3. Invest in a good storage system that makes tidying up easy and takes "stuff" out of sight. A famous large Swedish furniture store does a very inexpensive and sturdy range of shelves with interchangeable colourful plastic drawers.

4. Where possible, keep sleeping and playing areas separate, either in two separate rooms or within the room. This will make it easier for your child to sleep without distractions and wind down after the day.

5. Introduce routines and rituals from a young age. By that I mean simple predictable rituals such as getting up, mealtime and night time routines for example. Predictability is important for young children; it helps them feel safe and prevents unnecessary anxiety.

6. Try not to overload children with after-school activities (e.g. music lessons, sports training or scouts). Follow their lead and see what really interests them and what they enjoy doing, and limit these activities to one or two days a week. Children usually have a day packed full of activities in school and really benefit from spending time at home either by themselves or with friends and family.

Chapter 15

———

Creativity – the great opportunities and benefits of the arts

"All children are artists. The problem is how to remain an artist once he grows up."

PABLO PICASSO

WHAT IS ART?

The Oxford Dictionary defines art as, "The expression or application of human creative skill and imagination, typically in a visual form such as painting or sculpture, producing works to be appreciated primarily for their beauty or emotional power." The arts are the "various branches of creative activity, such as painting, music, literature and dance."

Art has been an innate part of human history and culture since the beginning of time. Art was used to make a mark before there were even rudimental forms of writing, and to this day there is evidence all over the world of the origins of human art. The 15,000-year-old Lascaux Caves in southwestern France, known as "the prehistoric Sistine Chapel", display some of the most remarkable Palaeolithic cave paintings in the world. Images depict hunting scenes and animals. Cueva de las Manos is a cave located in Patagonia in southern Argentina. It takes its name – Cave of the Hands – from the stencilled outlines of human hands, but it also displays other scenes. The Tadrart Acacus mountain range in the Sahara desert of western Libya is known for its rock paintings dating from 12,000 BC to 100 AD. The paintings reflect the changing environment of the Sahara desert, which used to have a very different climate: what is now desert had lakes and wooded areas with large herds of giraffes, elephants and ostriches. There are other artistic examples of human development just like these all over the world.

In my own personal view, the most magnificent pieces of art are created by Mother Nature herself; oftentimes, man-made art is replicating that which surrounds us. If you have ever walked on a deserted beach after the tide has gone out, you can see the most intricate and beautiful patterns in the undisturbed sand made by the flow of the water. Butterflies, birds and blossoms display the most wondrous vibrant colours, patterns and shapes. Crystals of incredible brilliance and colour are created in the depths of the earth. There is no end to the greatest of artists: Mother Earth. Even animals have a proclivity for the creation of art. The BBC documentary *Earth* celebrates one of nature's greatest artists: the Japanese Puffer Fish. To attract a mate, it works tirelessly for twenty-four hours a day for one week, creating a stunning sand mandala by just using its fins to plough through the sand with mathematical perfection. It even picks up shells to decorate this work of art.

Art is an invaluable part of the history of Earth and humanity, and it has been an integral part of culture, religion, psychology and the recording of historical events. It is basic human expression not only in the visual arts, but also in dance, music, literature and drama. Everybody has a creative part to their personality and that can mean a million different things for every person.

From my years teaching young children, I know of the big impact being creative has on young kids. You may say, "Well, my son never liked colouring in", or "My daughter's drawing skills leave much to be desired", but that is not the point. Maybe they simply love getting their hands messy from hand-printing. They might like cutting out cars and gluing them on cardboard. Perhaps they love modelling figurines from clay or stringing up pasta shapes to make bracelets or necklaces. Your child might be creative in making up their own songs or dances, or building musical instruments. Being creative has no limits and it can come in any shape or form ... literally! The arts and all of its aspects – such as the fun and enjoyment, the playful learning, the interaction and co-operation, the sensory impact, the self-expression, the being in the present moment when engaging in a creative activity – are so important for a child's sense of confidence, independence, self-awareness and pride. Every parent has seen that spark in their child's eye when they bring home a special painting or a handmade gift. They are thrilled and delighted to see their mum or dad's pride and happiness with the fruits of their creative heart and mind.

MUSIC

Whenever I see a documentary about indigenous people around the world, it strikes me how much more connected they are to music, dance and song. It seems to be a natural and integral part of their lives, firmly rooted in the expression of their inner feelings and emotions, their daily lives and rituals. It is a very direct form of non-verbal communication, the literal dancing and jumping for joy, the praising of gods, the giving thanks, the expression of deep grief and sorrow. Rather than self-consciously hiding behind others or being shy, children freely express themselves through song and dance. Often, there doesn't even seem to be formal routines but a natural flow of movement and expression.

Most parents, especially us mums, naturally and instinctively start singing lullabies to our children from the moment we know that they are growing in our womb. My second girl started to hum to herself from a very early age, before she could even mutter a simple word. She naturally used humming to soothe herself and was able to hum along with lullabies and simple songs before she started to talk. I have always been fascinated by the musical memory of humans. We are able to remember pieces of music, even if we haven't heard them in a long time. Despite not being able to formally read music, we can recall even complicated and intricate sequences.

Music is often a trigger for memories; we seem to be able to transport ourselves back to a certain time in our lives and even to a very specific moment and place. Music has the capacity to evoke feelings and emotions either through the memories recalled or by the musical content, melodies, lyrics and intricate compositions. As Bennett Reimer, a specialist in the philosophy of music education, explained in his 2004 paper "New Brain Research on Emotion and Feeling: Dramatic Implications for Music Education":

> That is what makes music so special, I propose: its endless capacity to expand the intricacies, depths, breadths, and diversities of conscious awareness, made available to our

minds and bodies through felt, sonic experience. Every musical experience that we have changes who we are. Although musical experience occurs in the present during which we are engaged in it, it also endures within us, in our brains and bodies.

One of the most fascinating experiences I have had with music, specifically singing, is the fact that people who have suffered a major stroke and have lost their ability to speak, sometimes will still be able to sing songs perfectly, as is the case with the mother of a good friend of mine.

Stephen Malloch in his article "Why do we like to dance and sing?" looked into some research to explore further why music is not just something humans love and enjoy; it is actually deeply rooted in our evolution. This means that music is an integral part of our humanity firmly intertwined into our very being. In his article he quotes Jon-Roar Bjørkvold who said, "To lose our musicality would be to lose a profound essential part of our humanity". John Blacking, one of the most influential ethnomusicologists of the twentieth century, believed that "The function of music is to enhance in some way the quality of individual experience and human relationships; its structures are reflections of patterns of human relations, and the value of a piece of music is inseparable from its value as an expression of human experience." The philosopher Roger Scruton points out that music still has the capacity to provide moral education: "Through melody, harmony and rhythm, we enter a world where others exist besides the self, a world that is full of feeling but also ordered, disciplined but free. That is why music is a character-forming force."

Children's first basic experience of music is the rhythmic beating of their mother's heart, the rhythm of her steps and movements. From inside the womb we are connected to melodies, beats, the rhythm of speech and song. Young children engage in musical activities with joy and natural enthusiasm. Early concepts are often taught through music and physical actions and dance, where learning is integrated in a more wholesome experience. Music connects us to others, to our environment, to spiritual experience, to joy, traditions and history and most importantly to ourselves. It is an integral part of us, and it is one part of the jigsaw that makes us human.

Especially in early education of children, irrespective of their abilities and needs, music is one of the primary and most successful methodologies for teaching basically anything. All parts of the curriculum integrate music: numbers, letters, shapes, colours, days of the week, months of the year, seasons, physical education, seasonal celebrations, body parts, nature etc. Topical content can be taught through singing, dancing, rhythmic exercises, rhyme, actions and using different kinds of instruments.

The Primary School Curriculum for Arts Education, as outlined by the government in 1999, gives the following background for the importance of music in a child-centred curriculum:

> Music is an indispensable part of the child-centred curriculum as one of the range of intelligences and as a special way of knowing and learning. Musical activity challenges the child to act in unique ways to listen discerningly to his/her own music and the music of others, to sing, play or read sensitively and accurately, and to evaluate critically. In posing these challenges, music contributes to the development of artistic awareness, self-expression, self-growth, self-esteem and multicultural sensitivity and, therefore, to the development of the whole child.
>
> An important aspect of music in the curriculum is the way it contributes to the personal, social, mental and physical development of the child. Coordination of mind and body is achieved through singing action songs, playing singing games, tapping rhythms, moving to music and playing in time while simultaneously listening to others, following directions or reading from notation.
>
> Speech development is fostered through working with vocal sounds, chanting, singing nursery rhymes and songs, experimenting with vowel and consonant sounds and learning to control breathing. Language development is enhanced through exposure to a wide variety of songs, containing new words, idioms and phrases. These words are used and extended in responding to music, describing sounds heard, feelings sensed, or stories related.
>
> The development of listening skills, a critical aspect of all learning, receives special attention through the exploration of sound and the identification of and discrimination between sounds in the environment, leading to increased sensitivity to musical works. Listening skills are also emphasised in performing and composing activities, where the development

of 'inner hearing' (or thinking in sound) is nurtured.

The development of both long-term and short-term memory occurs mainly, but not exclusively, through performing. Musical activities such as echo-singing and clapping develop short-term memory, while rote learning of songs, rhymes or games help to extend the capacity of long-term memory.

Opportunities to develop the imagination arise in unique ways in the music curriculum, through listening to familiar and unfamiliar musical works, hearing sounds internally, creating sound pictures or stories and expressing feelings and emotions in sound. This type of imaginative work also enhances spatial reasoning, which is the brain's ability to perceive the visual world accurately, to form mental images of physical objects, and to recognise variations in objects.

As a collaborative, interpersonal activity, music develops social skills through group performing or composing projects where ideas, instruments or specific skills are shared. It also provides opportunities for the development of lifelong leadership skills and fosters verbal and non-verbal communication. Music enhances the child's self-esteem through allowing him/her to see his/her own inventions valued and enjoyed by others, and to participate in singing games, songs, dances and group performances where each individual's contribution is vital to the group's success.

Music is an integral part of the child-centred curriculum, not just because it enhances other areas of learning but because it deepens the child's sense of humanity, teaching him/her to recognise beauty and to be sensitive to and to appreciate more fully the world in which he/she lives.

VISUAL ART

From a psychological point of view, art is an invaluable tool for non-verbal communication and expression. Pictures can say a thousand words and depending on the person, they can be the bridge to communication that spoken language, for whatever reason, can't provide in certain situations. For many years, psychologists, counsellors and educational professionals have used drawings to enable children to communicate feelings, experiences and certain issues and to support problem solving through the medium of art.

My eldest daughter, only a few mornings ago, woke up crying. She just couldn't verbalise what was wrong with her, only that she had had a bad dream. I didn't press the matter too much and just comforted her. As she loves drawing I gave her a pencil and a sheet of paper and encouraged her to draw what upset her so much in the dream. She sat down and drew a scene at a hospital: one child with chickenpox and one with a broken leg getting an injection s.a. All of a sudden she had no problem describing the scene to me, and her mood lifted instantly. Such is the significance of art in relation to working with children that the field of art therapy, which has developed since the late 1940s, has become an integral intervention when dealing with children's mental health. In recent years, an important focus has been put on the children's perspective and input regarding their works of art in order to get an insight into the personal meaning, rather than just the interpretation of "outsiders".

I recently watched a harrowing documentary about a residential weekend for children whose parents were the victims of murder or manslaughter. A crucial part of the intervention was an art-therapy session in which the children were supposed to draw a "comic-strip sequence" of their knowledge of what happened to their parents. My first reaction was pure horror at this suggestion, but as I watched the process it made perfect sense. Much of the children's trauma, apart from the obvious loss of their parent, stems from the "untold story" and probably parts they don't understand that keep ruminating in their heads. This causes additional suffering and confusion and if not treated will have a severe impact on the children's mental health. The format of the sequence rather than a single picture helped them to put a timeline and structure around their story. In their own words, the children then told the story with the help of their drawings and even though it was very tough to watch, the effect of this intervention was incredible. Children that hadn't cried since the event were able to open up and express their grief, and the sheer relief of being able to release their story was palpable.

Especially for children with special needs and communication deficits, pictures can enable first interactions and communication, and anybody who has ever been lucky enough to witness the powerful impact of these first steps will never forget it. One of the most frustrating things for many children with a communication delay is that they can't find an appropriate way to convey their most basic wants, needs and emotions. Unsurprisingly, this often leads to challenging behaviour. Imagine if you found yourself in a country where nobody spoke your language, where signs were written in letters you couldn't decipher. Now add to that an emergency of any kind, like simply needing to go to the toilet. Most of us might at least be able to use meaningful gestures, facial expression and other body language, but the inability to use spoken language would add a considerable amount of stress to even the simplest interaction. Once you have a scrap of paper and a pen, simple pictorials can convey a message in any language, which is one of the reasons many important signs (i.e. toilet, pharmacy, hospital, wheelchair access) are similar in most international countries.

Even from the point of view of expressing yourself emotionally, visual art gives countless opportunities. It's unimportant if a child is able to draw recognisable objects or people. Whether the child wishes to convey anger, happiness or excitement, expression through art can take on any form: slapping on paints with their hands; dancing through paint with their feet; gluing bits and pieces into collages; shaping clay or playdoh; blowing watercolours across a sheet of paper with a straw; ripping coloured card into shapes. The possibilities are endless and all provide an opportunity to enjoy the sensory experience through self-expression. I believe that there is a creative part in every human being. I'd even go so far as to say that the opportunity to be creative is a basic human need in order to be "whole". In the following section, I would like to give a little background on the use of mandalas as part of artistic expression, as it is that bit more specific to the area of formal mindfulness practice.

MANDALAS

"In the products of the unconscious we discover mandala symbols, that is, circular and quaternity figures which express wholeness, and whenever we wish to express wholeness, we employ just such figures."

CARL JUNG

I was first introduced to mandalas as a child, and at that time it was simply an exercise for colouring "within the lines" without any other meaning attached to it. Later, through my work as a teacher and my increased interest in mindfulness, spirituality, art and various meditative practices, I learned a little more about the origin, history and meaning of mandalas.

The word *mandala* is a Sanskrit term that means "circle" or "discoid object". A mandala can be defined in two ways: externally as a schematic visual representation of the universe, and internally as a guide for several psychophysical practices that take place in many Asian traditions, including meditation. Mandalas were originally objects of devotion in Tantric Hindu and Tantric Buddhism (Vajrayana Buddhism), and they are also used in Jainism. They can be painted on paper, wood, stone, cloth or even on a wall. In some traditions, they can be reproduced in ephemeral material such as butter or coloured sand. In Tibetan Buddhism, the role of mandalas is so strong that it could become an architectural structure and even whole temples may be built as giant mandalas.

Throughout the existence of humanity the "circle" has held great meaning, importance, satisfaction and also mystery. On a practical level, circular shapes, in particular the wheel, have basically shaped human development like nothing else. The wheel has influenced and continues to influence every single facet of society. Without wheels, transport, trade, travel, architecture, astronomy, farming, art, science, technology, sports etc. would not be what they are today.

On a more spiritual, artistic and historical level, mandalas are found among the most ancient art forms created by humans. As this subject is too vast and I simply want to include working with mandalas as part of a wholesome mindful approach, I have decided to just give a brief background and let you do further reading should you wish to. On their website, creatingmandalas.com, Susanne F. Fincher, Marilyn Clark and Susan Paul Johnson give a comprehensive background to mandalas, which I recommend for anybody interested in doing some further reading on this topic.

Cave paintings and rock carvings found all over the world depict the circular shape reflecting nature's cycles and shapes, such as day and night, the sun, moon and stars, birth, life and death, changing seasons and all that it entails, the moon phases and with it the changing of the tides.

Black Elk, the Dakota elder, beautifully expressed this all-encompassing view of a circular influence on every aspect of life, the world and the universe:

> Everything the Power of the World does is done in a circle. The sky is round, and I have heard that the earth is round like a ball, and so are all the stars. The wind, in its greatest power, whirls. Birds make their nests in circles, for theirs is the same religion as ours. The sun comes forth and goes down again in a circle. The moon does the same, and both are round. Even the seasons form a great circle in their changing, and always come back again to where they were. The life of a man is a circle from childhood to childhood, and so it is in everything where power moves.

The origin of mandalas (with the early depiction of a cross inside a circle) was probably connected to the human attempt to orient oneself in the world. As our ancestors attempted to make sense of their environment, they noticed that the horizon appeared to be a circle with them in the middle. In order to orientate their movements in large land areas, this depiction would have helped them to orientate themselves within their "world". It would have made sense to use the centre of the circle – oneself – as the focal point for a system of directions, for organising the space within the circle of the Earth's horizon.

The limbs create a right and left side. With arms outstretched in opposite directions away from the body, we might imagine lines extending beyond the outstretched arms to the horizon which establishes two opposite directions in the circle. The placement of the eyes in front of the head naturally suggests the line of sight as another direction, a line that would be continued in the opposite direction as well (backwards facing). These factors form a classic mandala pattern consisting of the horizon line (circle) and four lines radiating outward from the body in the centre.

Leonardo Da Vinci's *Vitruvian Man* illustrates this theory beautifully:

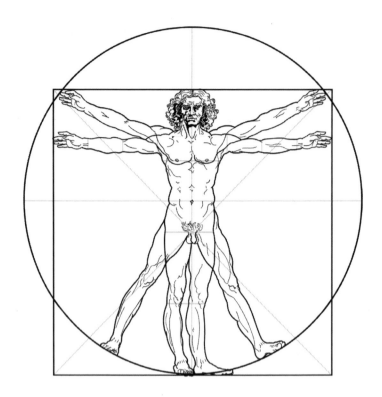

Encyclopaedia Britannica online states, "Leonardo envisaged the great picture chart of the human body he had produced through his anatomical drawings and Vitruvian Man as a *cosmografia del minor mondo* (cosmography of the microcosm). He believed the workings of the human body to be an analogy for the workings of the universe."

Cultural and historical landmarks all over the world and ancient mystical sites such as Stonehenge in England or Newgrange in Ireland are built and designed in a circular shape. Ancient calendars, such as the "Mayan Calendar Round" and the "Julian Calendar", compasses and clocks serve to illustrate the historically intrinsic meaning and importance of circles for humankind.

The famous Swiss psychiatrist Carl Gustav Jung defined mandalas as a centring process of the soul. Basically, he found that the composition of an external "order" will help connect to an inner balance resulting in inner peace and relaxation. He suggested that the mandala reflects our natural urge to live to our full potential – the circle being the symbol for our whole personality.

The benefits of mandalas in therapy, education and human development include:

- Learning to cope with rules and limits – to accept those that are necessary and to find the freedom to be creative in the spaces in-between.

- Connecting to your inner self – to find inner peace and rest within yourself.

- Centring and concentration alongside relaxation.

- Orientation within life's patterns.

- Better integration of experiences.

- Learning to get into resonance with a pattern.

- Developing towards a rounded, centred and full personality.

- Gaining strength from our centre/inner self.

Mandalas were/are used in many far Eastern traditions as meditation objects. Even though the origin of mandalas might have a religious background, they are now widely used as part of art education, relaxation approaches and meditation exercises. They are a valuable and enjoyable creative tool to use both in educational settings as well as at home and even for ourselves if we need a little creative time out.

"CRAFTING" AND MANUAL SKILLS – THE BENEFITS OF USING OUR HANDS

Creative thinking is at the root of modern-day innovation and invention. The dismissal of traditional skills and abilities while lauding only modern technology seems short-sighted. To deem manual skills and crafts unimportant while increasing our reliance on technology is risky. When was the last time you memorised an important telephone number or wrote a handwritten letter? Who has used an actual roadmap in recent years? Who has held an encyclopaedia in their hands and actually looked for information? When did you last fix a hole in a sock or jumper? Leaving the technology and information aspect to one side, children and adults now use their hands mostly for pressing buttons. This has a significantly detrimental effect on hand–eye coordination, fine motor skills and dexterity. Please don't get me wrong, I don't believe we should move backwards to living in caves and being hunter-gatherers, but why does it have to be an either/or?

Most crafts were born out of necessity, to fulfil basic human needs. They were the path towards innovation and industrialism. I am talking about crafts and "forgotten skills" that most people could do and which fulfilled both practical need and creativity. These include activities such as gardening, carving, weaving, pottery, cooking, baking, preserving, woodwork, foraging, sewing, knitting, simple construction skills and camping and "survival" skills. People were much more able to "help themselves" rather than having to rely on technology or a professional tradesperson when something went wrong. We now live in a disposable world where things are replaced rather than fixed, and we are sending out the wrong message to our children with this attitude. There have been increasing reports recently about the plastic pollution of our planet, particularly our oceans. In May 2017, the *Irish Independent* published an article about the uninhabited Henderson Island in the Pacific Ocean, which in 1988 was declared a World Heritage Site. It is the worst plastic-polluted place on Earth with 671 pieces of plastic per square metre! Not only are we suffocating our oceans and other eco-systems but there are also limited resources on this Earth. There will come a time, or should I say the time HAS come, when we need to rethink our habits if we want to secure a world worth living in for ourselves, our children and future generations.

Crafts are empowering skills for all of us with lots of advantages and benefits in many areas. They are an invaluable gift we should pass on to our children at home and should be established as a firm part of the school curriculum:

- We become more independent and skilful at making and repairing things rather than throwing them away. This provides a good example to our children and counteracts the pervasive "disposable" attitude.

- We improve hand–eye coordination, dexterity and fine motor skills.

- Especially for children, crafting encourages important visual-processing skills such as recognition of patterns, spatial rotation, geometrical shapes and sequences.

- Crafting is a multi-sensory experience, which in itself is an enjoyable process.

- We achieve a sense of pride, achievement and satisfaction by creating something.

- We gain a sense of security and independence as opposed to being dependent on technology or others.

- We improve our problem-solving skills.

- Crafts give a means of self-expression and creativity.

- By promoting crafts and forgotten skills we uphold our heritage and traditions. The UNESCO website states: "Traditional craftsmanship is perhaps the most tangible manifestation of intangible cultural heritage."

- Crafting and other traditional skills can be an important connection to our family history and even provide invaluable opportunities to connect the generations of a family. Children love to learn about their parents' and grandparents' lives, as my girls call it, "how things were done in the olden days".

From a mindfulness perspective, engaging in crafts pulls us into the present moment through focused attention – we become immersed in the activity and in that moment in time. Crafts are an opportunity for us parents and educators to connect with our children and co-operate in creating something. Any school subject can be integrated into crafting. Examples could include making puppets for storytelling (English), musical instruments (drama and music), constructing buildings or other objects with geometrical shapes (maths, social studies), building bird feeders or insect hotels as mentioned before (science); the opportunities are endless.

Chapter 16

 Connection and balance

Inever aspired to write a book; it was never one of my life goals. This book started out as something completely different – I initially started to compile a mindfulness programme for children. I decided to just "go with the flow", and after four years the jigsaw pieces became a whole. The experience was like a cathartic process in which I was able to organise my own priorities and beliefs, my hopes and worries, my past and present experiences, my practice and studies, in order to compile a guide, initially for myself, my parenting and teaching and my life in general. I know that experiences, life situations, beliefs and priorities are very different from person to person. Not everybody will share my viewpoints and that is only normal. If readers will be able to pick up just one or two helpful suggestions to make life easier, to contribute to a positive development within their families, then it was worthwhile. To sum up the essence of this book I want to put it very simply into these seven words: *It is all about connection and balance.*

CONNECTION:

- Connection to ourselves – to our body, heart, mind, soul, emotions, needs, passions and to our life purpose.

- Connection to our family, friends and neighbours – other human beings we meet in our daily interactions and beyond.

- Connection to our environment, home, neighbourhood,

school, town, country, nature and our pets – to the world we live in.

- Connection to our spirituality, whatever that means to each of us.

- Connection to our creativity and passion.

Balance: A healthy balance between "too much" and "too little" can be our goal regarding anything in life.

A mindful approach to life can support us in forming and maintaining these connections that give us a supported and secure place in our lives. When we bring more awareness into all of our daily interactions and surroundings, we are able to more easily assess what we (or others) need and re-evaluate our priorities and goals. When we stop functioning solely on autopilot and become more mindful, we can make healthier choices for our bodies, minds and our relationships; we can find a healthy balance.

Humans want and need to be and feel connected in order to find our own personal happy place in this world and to be part of the whole creation at the same time. The famous poem "No man is an Island" by John Donne from his *Meditation XVII – Devotions upon Emergent Occasions* was written nearly 400 years ago. However, it is still relevant today, as it beautifully illustrates the human longing for connection and belonging to "the main":

No Man is an Island
No man is an island entire of itself; every man
is a piece of the continent, a part of the main;
if a clod be washed away by the sea, Europe
is the less, as well as if a promontory were, as
well as any manner of thy friends or of thine
own were; any man's death diminishes me,
because I am involved in mankind.
And therefore never send to know for whom
the bell tolls; it tolls for thee.

Modern family life is very different from that of only a few decades ago. As well as the challenges and subsequent anxiety faced by parents and children that I have mentioned in previous chapters, there also seems to be a trend to "disconnect": a disconnection from human relationships, emotions, nature and basic necessary experiences. We have a responsibility as parents and educators to prepare our children for their future lives and to equip them with the necessary skills. We want to give them "roots to grow from and wings to fly". This does not mean that we have to "pre-cut" their lives and choices for them. Instead, we must help them learn skills that will enable them to make healthy and positive choices for themselves and to help them reconnect.

You might wonder if I am always mindful and present in every moment. Am I calm and collected, always kind and tolerant? Do I savour every bite I eat with full attention and gratitude? Do I always respond to negative emotions and stressful situations with a Zen-like attitude of non-judging and peaceful acceptance? Are my children always grateful for everything they receive, never whinge or get into fights with each other? Do my husband and I never argue, never snap at the girls because they have been asked to stop screeching for the tenth time? Can you guess the answer? It's NO – to all of the above. We are just a regular family facing our everyday struggles as well as we can. Some days we manage better than others, but every day is a new day, a new beginning. But the gift of mindfulness has been an invaluable companion and friend on the way. It helps us to cope better when the going gets tough. It reminds us of how lucky we really are. It pulls us right back out of our worrying heads into the here and now and the sensations in our bodies.

We should always remain realistic, as life will never go as planned. There will be many surprises, detours and disasters along the way for all of us, and oftentimes we won't initially have the solutions for ourselves or our children. There are no perfect parents or perfect parenting, and we should not be our worst enemies by expecting unrealistic outcomes. Sometimes we will hit a wall and all the good intentions of "mindful interactions" will go out the window for that moment as we find ourselves shouting at ourselves and others. Sometimes we will feel helpless, overwhelmed and frustrated, and we will resign ourselves to not having the answers we hoped for. Situations will arise that will challenge us to the core. Family structures can change through unforeseen circumstances; factors beyond our control can arrive like a whirlwind and reorganise everything beyond recognition. That's just life, and everybody will have times in their lives when things just don't go to plan. With regular practice of mindfulness though, be it formal or integrated into everyday interactions, we will have a valuable tool to catch ourselves, our thoughts, our emotions and our physical sensations and pull ourselves back into that very moment. By becoming aware of our bodies and our breath and by applying the mindful attitudes especially of non-judging, patience, kindness, trust and acceptance to ourselves and others, we will be able to become aware of things as they really are, which will help us to make more informed and healthier choices for ourselves and our families.

When children are introduced to a more mindful lifestyle from a young age, these strategies and lifestyle choices may become naturally integrated into their interactions and relationships and will hopefully contribute to a happy, wholesome and connected life with roots to grow from and wings to fly.

Last but not least, I want us all, parents and educators, to enjoy "our" children and their childhood and help them make precious memories which will stay with them for a lifetime. I frequently encounter older people reminding us to "enjoy them while they are young" because "they grow up much too quickly, so make the most of it". Childhood is precious and life is short; it's not a dress rehearsal. A friend of mine recently told me about a very touching chat she had with her dad. He told her that if he had one wish, he would wish to spend one week with his six daughters when they were little. The following poem by Lucy Berry sums it up beautifully:

The Last Time

The father, reading to his girl
some little tale they always read
is unaware that this may be
the last one that she'll ever need;
she's grown past stories softly read
by daddy sitting on the bed.

The mother with her muddy son,
kicking a football in the park,
cannot sense as they wander home
through chilly, soft-approaching dark;
this was the last time they'd come out
to kick that happy ball about.

How secret, sneaky-soft they come:
those last times when we'll kiss it better,
hold their hand across the road
or lift them up to post a letter.
They pass unmarked, un-noticed; for
we're not so needed any more.

So they abandon fairy tales,
and nursery rhymes that mummy sings
and leave behind soft toys — and us —
and put away their childish things;
a loss so small. Our loss the greater,
unmissed, un-mourned, until years later.

So jump in muddy puddles, build sandcastles, roll around in the grass, bake cupcakes, have pillow fights and teddy bears' picnics. Treasure every kiss and cuddle! Treasure childhood and parenthood! It won't last forever, and in the blink of an eye we will be the ones reminding young mums and dads to savour every minute of being a parent to young children.

Wishing us all more kindness, peace, health, love, well-being and treasuring the time with our children!

Part 2

Practical Tips, Ideas and Exercises

———————

I n this more "hands-on" section, I want to give you some ideas and impulses for activities, resources and exercises or even just thoughts for integrating the different topics of the previous chapters into everyday life, either at home or in educational and caregiving settings. As all of these areas by their very nature can't be seen in isolation, many of the activities are touching on multiple topics. I have tried my best to divide them into categories for ease of use but you will often find that activities may also fit into other sections and can be used at your discretion. I hope that you will find some of these ideas useful and easy to include into your everyday routine. After a while they can become a natural part of your interactions, and you will see positive changes in yourself, your children and interactions beyond the home.

1. INTENTIONALITY AND MINDFUL PARENTING

Intentionality – Parenting as a Spiritual Discipline (from Everyday Blessings *by Myla and Jon Kabat-Zinn):*

Intentions remind us of what is important. When we form the intention to do something, and that intention informs our choices and our actions, the chances that we will be sensitive to what is important in our lives increase greatly, and we are more likely to see the big picture. Our intentions serve as blueprints, allowing us to give shape and direction to our efforts and to assess how we are doing as we work at developing something worthy of ourselves and our lives. So at some point, whenever that is, we have to decide what is really important to us, and we must strive constantly to keep that framework in mind as things unfold.

In mindful parenting, certain principles are important to affirm from the very beginning. This does not mean that if we already have children it is too late to become more mindful in our parenting. It means that we begin when we are ready, wherever we are in our lives, and work with the here and now, formulating the intentions that are important for us to affirm and to implement. We should also be realistic. It is never too late to introduce mindfulness into our lives, and the very moment that we make the conscious commitment to do so becomes the perfect moment to begin.

Here are some intentions that you may find helpful. Of course you can also create your own.

> *Intention One*: I will bring my entire creative genius to the work of mindful parenting.

> *Intention Two*: I will see parenting as a spiritual discipline, meaning that it provides me with every necessary opportunity to cultivate wisdom and openheartedness in myself, so that I may come to know and express my true nature and share what is best in me with my children and with the world.

> *Intention Three*: I will cultivate mindfulness and discernment in my daily life, especially with my children, using an awareness of my breathing to ground me in the present moment.

> *Intention Four*: I will make every effort to see who my children actually are, and to remember to accept them for who they are at every age, rather than being blinded by my own expectations and fears. By making a commitment to live my own life fully and to work at seeing and accepting myself as I am, I will be better able to accord a similar acceptance to my children. In this way I can help them to grow and to realise their full potential as unique beings.

Intention Five: I will make every effort to see things from each child's point of view, understand what my children's needs are and to meet them as best I can.

Intention Six: I will use whatever comes up in my own life and in the lives of my children, including the darkest and most difficult times, as "grist to the mill", to grow as a human being so that I am better able to understand my children, their soul needs, and what is required of me as a parent.

Intention Seven: I will fold these intentions into my heart and commit myself to putting them into practice as best I can, every day, and in appropriate ways that feel right to me and that honour my children's sovereignty, and my own.

Twelve exercises for mindful parenting, from Everyday Blessings *by Myla and Jon Kabat-Zinn:*

1. Try to imagine the world from your child's point of view, purposefully letting go of your own. Do this every day for at least a few moments to remind you of who this child is and what he or she faces in the world.

2. Imagine how you appear and sound from your child's point of view; imagine having you as a parent today, in this moment. How might this modify how you carry yourself in your body and space, how you speak, what you say? How do you want to relate to your child in this moment?

3. Practise seeing your children as perfect just the way they are. Work at accepting them as they are when it is hardest for you to do so.

4. Be mindful of your expectations of your children, and consider whether they are truly in your children's best interests. Also, be aware of how you communicate those expectations and how they affect your children.

5. Practise altruism, putting the needs of your children above your own whenever possible. Then see if there isn't some common ground where your needs can also be met. You

may be surprised how much overlap is possible, especially if you are patient and strive for balance.

6. When you feel lost, or at a loss, remember to stand still. Meditate on the whole by bringing your full attention to the situation, to your child, to yourself, to the family. In doing so, you may go beyond thinking and perceive intuitively, with the whole of your being, what really needs to be done.

7. Try embodying silent presence. Listen carefully.

8. Learn to live with tension without losing your own balance. Practise moving into any moment, however difficult, without trying to change anything and without being blinded by a particular desired outcome. See what is "workable" if you are willing to trust your intuition and best instincts.

9. Apologise to your child when you have betrayed a trust in even a little way. Apologies are healing, and they demonstrate that you see a situation more clearly or more from your child's point of view. But "I'm sorry" loses its meaning if we are always saying it, or if we make regret a habit.

10. Every child is special, and every child has special needs. Each sees in an entirely unique way. Hold an image of each child in your heart. Drink in their being, wishing them well.

11. There are very important times when we need to practise being clear, strong and unequivocal with our children. Let this come as much as possible out of awareness, generosity and discernment, rather than out of fear, self-righteousness or the desire to control. Mindful parenting does not mean being overindulgent, neglectful or weak; nor does it mean being rigid and controlling.

12. The greatest gift you can give your child is your self. This means that part of your work as a parent is to keep growing in self-knowledge and in awareness. We have to be grounded in the present moment to share what is deepest and best in ourselves.

2. How to explain mindfulness to children

The concept of "mindfulness" can be quite abstract to grasp, even for us adults. I remember listening to a recording of Sogyal Rinpoche at a meditation retreat. He compared mindfulness meditation and the calming of a busy mind with the image of a glass of dirty water that had just been stirred. We were to visualise this glass of water and imagine how the dirt would settle in the glass after a little while. Even though this is many years ago, it is still my strongest image of what mindfulness is to me. It is important to use age-appropriate and easily understandable language and metaphors/pictures when explaining mindfulness to children. The following activities will help children understand what mindfulness is:

Busy mind, peaceful mind

This exercise is based on the above example by Sogyal Rinpoche. You can use this in a group/class setting or at home with your own children.

1. For this beautiful illustration of the meaning of a busy mind and a peaceful mind, pour some water into a clear container such as a glass or a jug. Ask children to look at the container and describe what they can see.

2. After a minute sprinkle some fine sand or glitter into the glass or jug and stir with a wooden spoon or stick.

3. Again ask participants what they see.

4. Explain that this is what happens in their mind when they are worried, angry, distracted, stressed out or agitated and their thoughts and feelings are all muddled up in their heads.

5. Stop stirring. Guide the children to keep observing the water in the glass/jug to see what happens as the sand or glitter settles to the bottom.

6. Explain to them that that's what mindful breathing does to their minds. It settles and calms their mind, slows down their thoughts and feelings, and helps them to feel more relaxed and able to concentrate.

7. Then tell them to wiggle their body to get their mind revved up again while stirring the water or adding more sand or glitter.

8. Show them how cloudy the water is again – like their mind when it's busy – and watch it settle as they sit quietly, breathing and watching. Ask them to raise their hand when they can see through the water again.

9. Ask them to breathe slowly as they watch the water clear. Explain that by breathing slowly and steadily into their belly, their thoughts and feelings settle and their minds become calm and clear.

There are many variations to this exercise that you can use e.g. a snow glass, sensory glitter cone, simple plastic bottle filled with water and sand or glitter etc. You could also make it into an interactive activity, giving every participant a glass with water, a spoon and some sand or glitter.

Be the pond

A teacher developed this story/exercise to explain a "busy mind", to help name emotions and thoughts and to watch them pass by.

Let the children sit down in a comfortable position and close their eyes. Suggest they do some mindful breathing first. Now let them visualise a pond with lots of fish swimming in it. All the fish have different feelings and emotions. Some are happy and relaxed, some are sleepy, some are quite sad, others are really angry etc. All of them move with different speed and movement through the pond. Let the children look at the different faces and facial expressions. Name the different emotions they can see. Now encourage the children to imagine them being the pond, not the fish.

In a more practical exercise, you could use the worksheet included in the appendix as an art activity, especially for younger children who might find visualisations too challenging. Let children draw in facial expressions for each fish and colour them in. You could let them cut the fish out and stick them onto a blue sheet of paper or even use a larger display board for a "communal" pond. Adapt it in whatever way is suitable for your children, and be creative.

3. How to explain the brain and mindfulness to children

In his article "The Mindful Brain – Mindfulness and the brain – How to explain it to children", Chris Bergstrom gives the following child friendly version of what happens in our brains when we apply mindfulness:

"The Amygdala – The Jumpy Superhero"

The amygdala is like the brain's superhero, protecting us from threats. It helps us to react quickly when there is danger. Sometimes it's good to react – when there's a real physical threat, like when you see a football coming your way. The amygdala simply decides that there's not enough time to think about it and makes us react quickly: you move your head away from the path of the football. In this way, the amygdala can decide whether we get to think about the information our body gathers through our senses or not.

But there's a problem. The amygdala can't see a difference between real danger and something stressful. You could say it's jumpy and that it makes mistakes. When we're angry, sad or stressed the amygdala thinks there's real imminent danger. We then simply react without thinking. We might say or do something we regret immediately. We might even start a fight or just freeze when we're offended, or supposed to take a test or speak in front of the class. Fear and stress shuts down our thinking in this way.

"The Prefrontal Cortex – The Smart One"

The part of our brain that helps us make good choices is called the prefrontal cortex, or PFC. You could call it the smart one, as it helps you make smart choices and decides what is stored in your memory.

To make good choices, the PFC needs to get the information our body gathers through the senses – sights, sounds, smells and movements. The question is: will the amygdala allow the PFC to analyse the information early enough?

Remember: the amygdala, the jumpy superhero, oftentimes hinders the information from going to the prefrontal cortex and we make rash choices. This can happen when we're angry, sad, negative, stressed or anxious. What we want to do is to help the jumpy superhero calm down. But how?

Here's the trick:

When we're calm, the amygdala is calm and sensory information flows to the prefrontal cortex and we can make better choices. Even our memory improves when we're calm and happy. We're able to remember better and make new, lasting memories. So, how do we calm down to help the PFC, the smart one, have time to get and analyse all the information for us so that we make better choices?

Mindfulness practice to the rescue

Mindfulness helps us to calm down, and this, in turn, calms the amygdala so that it allows the information flow to the prefrontal cortex – that part of our brains that helps us make good choices. When we're calm, we can more easily be mindful and make good choices. Scientists have figured out that the prefrontal cortex is more activated following mindfulness training and our high-level functions like the intention to pay attention, emotional regulation, body regulation, our communication skills, empathy, and our ability to calm and self-soothe are more available to us. Pretty cool, right? The more we practise mindfulness the more we'll experience calm moments, even if we weren't trying to be mindful.

How can I do this?

1. When you feel overwhelmed, stop for a moment, take a few deep breaths and exhale slowly. Name the emotion you are experiencing.

2. Focus on your breath for five breaths. See where you can feel your breath most easily – your stomach, your chest or your nose.

3. Control your breathing for a short while. Do deep belly breathing for five breaths. Put your hands on your belly and feel how it expands as you breathe in.

4. Multiple short mindful moments per day trains your brain to become more mindful even when you don't

try to be mindful. In other words, the more you train, the easier it will be to be mindful and self-soothe when you're actually in a stressful situation.

4. HOW TO EXPLAIN NEUROPLASTICITY TO CHILDREN

I really like these following exercises from Debra Burdick's book, *Mindfulness Skills for Kids and Teens*:

Neuroplasticity: like paths in the grass or sand

1. If possible, take children outside onto a lawn or a sandy beach (preferably undisturbed, without marks or footprints).

2. Bring their attention to the grass/sand and how it looks.

3. Ask them to walk in a straight line across the grass/sand. Do it with them.

4. Now look at the grass/sand and ask if they can see where they walked.

5. Walk back and forth several times until they can see where the grass/sand is beginning to get matted down.

6. Ask them if they have ever seen a path worn in the grass right down to the dirt. Show them one if possible.

7. Ask them what happens if no one walks on the path anymore.

8. Explain that this is like the process of neuroplasticity in the brain. According to Hebb's axiom, neurons that fire together wire together, and dendrites increase in size and efficiency when something is repeated over and over. So, simply put, like the path worn in the grass or sand, the neuronal pathway gets stronger and stronger with repetition and weaker and weaker with disuse.

Mindfulness practice can help rewire the brain and is an effective way to create more healthy "pathways" and connections in the brain.

Neuroplasticity exercises indoors

Worn–path visualisation:

1. Close your eyes and picture a lawn of green grass.

2. Now imagine that someone walks across the grass diagonally from one corner of the lawn to the opposite corner.

3. Notice how the grass changes. Perhaps the grass is a bit matted down where they walked.

4. Now imagine lots of people walking across the grass following the same path.

5. After a while, notice that some of the grass is dying, where so many footsteps have fallen.

6. Imagine that this process continues until there is a path worn in the lawn where there is no longer any grass – just a dirt path worn smooth from all the foot traffic.

7. Now imagine the lawn with the path across it. Notice what happens to it over time when no one walks on it anymore. The grass slowly starts to grow where the path was until at some point there is no longer a path at all.

Mindfulness practice can help rewire the brain so it no longer automatically responds with anxiety or anger, fear or feeling stressed. Mindfulness helps to decrease the negative pathways in the brain and increases healthier, more integrated connections.

Paper-folding exercise:

1. Give participants a piece of heavy paper.

2. Ask them to fold the paper in half, then fold it again, and then again. Do it with them. Guide them to press down on the fold to sharpen it. Encourage them to notice how difficult or easy it is to fold the paper each time.

3. Have them unfold it and fold it again where it was already folded.

4. Ask them if refolding is faster and easier than folding the paper in the first place.

5. Relate this to moving information along a well-travelled path of neurons.

6. Discuss whether it is easier for your brain to think something new or the same thought.

7. Ask them if it is easier to learn something new or do something you have done before.

5. KINDNESS ACTIVITIES

Kindness is essential for our happiness – be it kindness towards others, kindness towards our environment or most importantly kindness towards ourselves. I love Eline Snell's description of kindness in her book, *Sitting Still Like a Frog*:

> Kindness is one of the most powerful qualities a person can possess. It is like a gentle rain that falls everywhere, without excluding a single place. It just falls without distinction. Kindness is non-judgemental and inclusive – that is if it is genuine. Kindness touches your heart, enabling you to grow and learn to trust yourself and others. Kindness towards yourself and others comforts, heals and helps you to be more balanced and open, even when things are difficult and distressing.

Kindness can be included in so many small ways into our daily routines and interactions. The most important thing to keep in mind is trying our best to give a good example. Everybody gets angry or frustrated sometimes and that is only normal. But if we can try and include kindness as a natural "default mode" we can't go wrong. Be kind to yourself, be kind to the people you meet, be kind to the cat and the dog, be kind to the tree and the flower. As soppy as it may sound, if we try to apply a kind attitude towards everything around us this will also reflect back on ourselves.

Here are some more practical exercises and activities that can be included to involve children in the "kindness revolution":

Kindness brainstorming

Before we can teach children about kindness we need to find out what they believe kindness is and what their experiences are. Let them think about it for a few minutes or introduce the topic with a short story about kindness. Ask the child/children: Can you think of something that happened recently where you were shown kindness by somebody, or where you showed kindness to somebody else? Give examples of what you think is kind/an act of kindness.

Intention of kindness

It is great to start our day with a positive intention, both for ourselves as well as our children. Think about a kind intention for the day. This can be a very small and simple thing that could make a big difference to somebody including ourselves.

    Today I am going to:
- Help Mum with the washing-up without being asked.
- Give Dad a hug out of the blue.
- Greet everyone I meet with a smile.
- Try not to waste water.

Random act of kindness

This is similar to the above exercise but can be a more specific thing to do and might take a little more planning and even parental or teacher's help. Children can come up with their own ideas, and it could be a weekly or even monthly activity to keep it motivating and realistic to carry out. The possibilities are endless and children can be as creative as they like.

    Today I/we will:
- Sort out my toys and pick some that we could bring to a day-care centre.
- Share some of my pocket money.
- Buy some groceries and drop them to the local soup kitchen.
- Write a card to a friend or relative we haven't spoken to in a while.
- Drop in a piece of cake to an elderly neighbour.

In schools this activity can be a little more structured. In a brainstorming exercise pupils can come up with their ideas of "small acts of kindness". They can all be written down and displayed on a board, and every day one pupil can take their turn to pick an act of kindness and carry it out.

Circle of kindness

This is a lovely circle time routine for schools, pre-schools or other childcare settings. In order for no child to be left out and to avoid children just picking their best friends, all the names are written on a small piece of paper, folded and placed into a hat or something similar. The first child picks out a name and says something nice about this person and hands the hat to the next child and so on. To make verbalising easier for younger children you could stick to a certain phrase such as: "I like you because ..." or "My favourite thing about you is ..." See what's most suitable in your circumstances.

"Star Thrower" activity

Read the short, adapted story of the "Star Thrower" that appears in chapter six. I have also included a template in the appendix. Encourage the children to be "star throwers" and think of a small act of kindness. Give every child a photocopy of the starfish also included in the appendix and let them colour in the starfish and write down their kind idea. Cover a display board or large piece of cardboard with blue paper symbolising the ocean and pin on all the ideas. Let the board be their inspiration for small acts of kindness to brighten up somebody's day.

Kindness challenge

Either at home or in school, set your child/children a kindness challenge for the week. You can use the sheet with various acts of kindness included in the appendix, see what happened at the end of the week and chat about the experience.

Kindness Post-it notes (see templates)

Randomly write a nice Post-it note for a member of your family, a friend, a neighbour etc. and stick it in an unexpected space where they will find it. This is a great way to put a smile on someone's face.

Pay it forward

I recently read about a beautiful idea: the "pay-it-forward coffee". People go into a café or restaurant and pay in advance for a coffee that somebody who mightn't have enough money can get for "free". I love this idea of paying forward, and I think we can all do variations of this idea. It doesn't have to be a coffee; it could be a bun, a chocolate bar or a drink – anything at all. It is another example of that beautiful sentiment: "A simple act of kindness will have an endless ripple."

"Friendship/Kindness Pebbles"

For this group activity, give every child a nice smooth pebble about the size of the palm of their hand. This exercise is a "child friendly" variation of a loving-kindness meditation, and its purpose is to connect to the heart and mind and to send out positive, affirming and kind messages. This will have a positive impact on the sender as well as the recipient.

For a few minutes let them hold the pebble and focus their awareness on its shape, texture, colour and unique features. Tell them that these are special friendship/kindness pebbles that have to be programmed with kind wishes and affirmations for somebody else. The children don't know who will receive their special pebble as the "gifting process" will be done anonymously. Give every child a sheet of paper and encourage them to write down five kind wishes or nice affirmations for the person who will receive the pebble. Depending on the setting, children might find this challenging initially. Give them some examples such as:

– "I wish you health and happiness."
– "I wish you good friends."
– "You are a lovely person!"
– "You are beautiful!"

When the children are finished writing, tell them that now they have to programme the pebble with their positive messages. Ask them to hold the pebble, really look at it and put their messages into it, saying them loudly or internally. The important thing is to really connect to their heart, to really mean what they are saying. When they have done this let children wrap the note around the pebble with a nice ribbon and place them into a box or canvas bag.

The gifting of the pebbles can be done in different ways: two classes could exchange their pebbles; children in the same class could pick a pebble each blindfolded; the children could enclose a pebble in a Christmas Appeal box or donate them to a homeless charity. The options are endless, and it is a nice way of spreading kindness and happiness.

6. EXERCISES TO PROMOTE TOLERANCE

As outlined in Part 1 of this book, we live in times when, more than ever, it is essential that we promote tolerance and acceptance of all of our differences, big and small, to ensure an inclusive and peaceful society. Young children are free of judgement, racism and prejudice, and if we as parents and educators meet them right there and help them to continue this attitude, we can't go wrong. We also won't need to reverse or reshape learned behaviours but can build on our children's positive social outlook; we could even learn from them.

Bullying is a real and worrying issue in our schools and society, and modern phenomena such as social media have greatly accelerated its impact. While promoting tolerance towards diversity, it is imperative that we educate our children early about bullying. How do you recognise it and what do we do when we see it happening?

Exercise to explain the effects of bullying to children

Apple exercise

Take a beautiful unmarked apple and give it to a child or student in your class to hold. Now ask the child to throw the apple on the floor, making sure it doesn't get completely smashed, just slightly bruised. Ask the child to pick up the apple and hit it on a table, again, just enough to bruise it slightly. Repeat a few times. Ask the child to hold up the apple and say: "Sorry". Repeat a couple of times. Now let the child/children observe the apple. What does it look/feel like? Will the apple ever be "whole" again? Take the apple and cut it in half. Let children voice their observations. What does the apple look like in the inside?

Now explain that this is what happens when a child is bullied. Even if you say sorry a few times, the child will always carry the scars and bruises inside them. They will never completely heal or forget.

Paper exercise

Give the child/children a new sheet of paper and ask them to crunch it up into a ball. Ask them to throw it onto the floor and stamp on it repeatedly but trying not to rip it at the same time. Ask the children to unfold and smooth the paper as best they can and observe. What does the paper look like? Is it dirty, damaged or creased? Now let the children "apologise" and say sorry to the piece of paper. Do this a few times. What does the paper look like now? Is it still the same? As above, explain that this is what happens when a child is bullied. The child, as the paper, will never be the same, and in some cases will remain badly damaged and affected by bullying.

We're all the same on the inside

This could be an exercise integrated into a cookery lesson or making a cake for a celebration. You need some white and some brown eggs for this activity and you can vary the approach depending on age etc. Either the teacher/parent cracks the eggs into one big bowl or older children can crack one white and one brown egg into their own bowls. Ask the children if they can see a big difference between the eggs in the bowl. In a variation, one child cracks the two eggs into two separate little bowls and another child has to guess which one was the brown egg and which was the white egg. It's just a simple exercise to illustrate that we might all be visually different on the outside, but we all have hopes and dreams, we all want to fit in, we all want to be loved and are somewhat the same on the inside.

Again there are many variations to this. You could peel different coloured apples, squeeze different sizes of oranges, chop big and small tomatoes etc.

Exercise to illustrate prejudice

The presents

I read about this activity a number of years ago, and I adapted the exercise because I couldn't exactly remember relatives and presents mentioned in the original instructions. This can be done as either an individual or group activity, and it can be adapted for different age groups or settings. Don't be afraid to be creative. An example of a set of instructions is as follows:

1. Participants are asked to choose presents for four relatives: Uncle Mick, a builder; Aunt Cathy, a housewife; Cousin Luke, a musician; and Cousin Amy, a teenager.

2. "You can choose one present each from the following eight presents:
   Electric drill, cookbook, tickets to the opera, rock music CD, marshmallows, travel guide for Africa, hammock, voucher for a beautician."

3. Once the children have picked the presents let them announce and explain why they picked the presents for the person.

4. Now give the children the following facts about the four relatives:

   a. Uncle Mick is taking a year off to travel around Africa, which has always been his dream. His favourite sweets are marshmallows.

   b. Aunt Cathy builds beautiful wooden furniture as a hobby while listening to her favourite rock bands.

   c. Luke loves to cook for family and friends and likes getting a massage when his shoulders are tense from practising the piano.

   d. Amy plays the violin and loves going to the opera. She would love a hammock for her favourite spot in the garden to read her books.

5. Discuss

We're all different and the same

This exercise can be done with a partner or by yourself. Either think of another person, anybody at all, or use your partner as an example. With a simple Venn diagram (two interlinked circles) note three things that you have in common and three things that are different. This is a great tool to illustrate that even though everybody is unique, we all have many things in common, no matter where we come from, what religion we practise, what age we are etc.

What would our community look like without diversity?

In a brainstorming session encourage children to list the influence of cultural and national diversity in their community and their immediate environment. Write down all the different examples such as a Chinese restaurant, pizza, curry, clothes manufactured overseas, movies and television programmes, music, any other products in the shops produced in various countries, friends and family with different nationalities etc. Now ask children to imagine their surroundings without any of these things. Would it be better or would they miss these things?

Tolerance and experience of disabilities

With this type of activity children can experience, even for a few minutes, what it would be like to live with a certain disability. This encourages them to "put themselves in someone else's shoes" and get an insight, even just a little glimpse, into their experience of life. This exercise can be introduced in many different ways: blindfold children and let them carry out a simple everyday task such as drawing a picture to experience blindness; let children try and move around in a wheelchair; instruct them to wear ear defenders during class and try to follow the lesson for a few minutes etc. There are many possibilities in which we can encourage our children to see the world through someone else's eyes.

7. BREATHING EXERCISES

Opening the throat

Many people constrict their throats when they are feeling nervous, upset, or excited. A closed throat can make exercising, using the voice, and even breathing difficult. This exercise helps participants recognise what a relaxed, open throat feels like.

Have the group sit in a circle and help them loosen their neck and shoulder muscles with a few warm-ups. You might have them tense their shoulders, raising them up to the ears, and then relax them. Now ask the participants to yawn; encourage them to notice how their throats feel when they yawn. Tell them that this is the feeling of an open throat.

Next ask everybody to sit up as tall as possible. They should imagine someone pulling the crown of their heads with a string. Have them say "hah" softly with an open throat. As participants vocalize, have them drop their heads down to their chest, and then bring them back up. Then have them drop their heads backwards and to each side, bringing the head back to the centre each time. Ask them how the positions feel different. Help them recognise that bending the neck constricts the throat, and that the throat is most open in the centre position. Point out how standing straight can help with breathing freely.

FROM *Yoga Games for Children*, DANIELLE BERSMA & MARJOKE VISSCHNER

Mindful breathing

Mindful breathing is one of the basic "formal" mindfulness exercises. This practice involves intentionally focusing on our breathing. This isn't as easy as you might initially think, however, it becomes second nature when practised regularly. Mindful breathing is an invaluable tool to calm ourselves in difficult situations.

- To practise mindful breathing it can help to sit or lie down, but if that isn't possible it is also fine to practise standing up.

- First of all we bring our attention to our body and focus on the parts that are involved in breathing. Feel the air streaming in through the nostrils or mouth and feel our chest and belly rise and fall.

- We should not try too hard to change our natural breath, but it can be helpful to breathe into our belly and become aware of its rising and falling.

- Our minds will wander and thoughts will enter our heads; that's what our minds do. Just notice the thoughts without any judgement and bring your attention back to your breath again and again. It is sometimes easier to bring back the focus by using words for our breathing, which we can say internally: "Breathing in … breathing out", "in … out", "one, two, three, four … one, two, three, four". Find whatever suits you and your breathing.

This exercise can be used as a quick "breathing space" even just for a couple of minutes, or you can use it regularly at a certain time of the day for fifteen minutes or more to recharge your batteries and come back into the present.

Children often find breathing exercises quite challenging initially, as their body awareness isn't developed fully yet. That is why initially it is a good idea to use the "breathing aids" outlined below for younger children.

Breathing up into the sky and down into the earth

A great breathing-exercise helper for children (and adults) is physical movement. In this breathing exercise children should stand upright and have enough space around them so they don't touch anybody or anything with stretched-out arms. Participants can close their eyes or keep them open if they find it difficult to balance with their eyes closed. Ask children to let their arms hang loosely on their sides and even shake them a little to ease any tension. Next instruct children to breathe in slowly and with the in-breath raise their arms "up into the sky", stretching upwards as high as they can, giving their whole body a nice extension. Pause for a moment and ask them to breathe out slowly, moving the arms back down with the out-breath. Once children are familiar with the movement you can vary the instructions, such as the following, or make up your own:

– "Breathe in up into the sky."
– "Breathe out down into the earth."

Or,

– "Breathe in happiness, love and kindness."
– "Breathe out worries, fears and tension."

Starfish breathing stretch

The idea for this lovely breathing exercise is from Susan Kaiser

Greenland's fantastic book, *The Mindful Child*. Before the exercise, or even integrated into a science lesson or the "Star Thrower" story, tell the children a little bit about starfish. Starfish have five limbs which are arranged around a centre disk. At the end of each limb they have a simple eye that can't see too clearly but can sense light and darkness. Starfish do most things from their centre. Now let children lie down and stretch out their five limbs (including their head and neck) without touching anything around them. Ask children to focus on their starfish centre (abdomen) and take a deep breath into it. Say the following: "While breathing in stretch out all of your limbs and then relax breathing out." Repeat this exercise a few times. This is a great activity to settle children and become calm. The physical and imaginary aspect helps young children especially to focus and follow the instructions.

Duck on the water

It can be challenging for children to have the body awareness for abdominal breathing. There are lots of ways in which we can help them to direct their breathing and be aware of it. Give children a rubber duck. Let them lie on their backs and place the duck on their tummies. Now the ducks want to ride the waves in the lake. The waves go up and down, up and down with their breathing. Watch the little duck as it bops up and down on the water. You can adapt this exercise any way you like. Use teddies as "breathing buddies"; beanbags are another option.

Blowing bubbles

Something as simple as blowing bubbles can bring children's attention to their breathing. To help children focus on their actual breath, give them small verbal impulses such as: "breathing in ... breathing out". Once children have practised with real bubbles you can use this activity at any stage even without bubble mixture at hand. Just ask the child to raise two fingers to their mouth to symbolise the bubble wand and give the same instructions: "breathing in ... breathing out" or "breathing in ... blowing bubbles".

Breathing beads

Sometimes children need something they can literally grasp, in order to help them understand a concept and follow an instruction. The concept of mindful breathing can be very difficult for young children as body awareness is not fully developed yet. These little helpers are easily made and can make a big difference for simple breathing breaks. They can be kept in a coat pocket and be always available when needed, like a little talisman.

You need a relatively thick and soft string and about twelve smooth wooden beads. Match them in a way that when threaded the beads aren't too loose but glide along easily. Thread the first bead and tie a knot so beads won't fall off and then thread the rest of the beads. Tie the last bead with a knot at the other end of the string so you have two stoppers at either end. The finished bead string should be about 20–25 cm long depending on the thickness of the beads.

Let children push all beads to one side and then instruct them to take a breath in, while they move the first bead slowly to the other end. Breathe out with the second bead and so on. It takes a couple of attempts to find a good "rhythm", but once kids get used to their breathing beads it can be a great tool for mindful breathing exercises.

Breathing pebbles

This little helper can make a big difference in prompting small breathing breaks throughout the day. Find a nice pebble on the beach or by a river and decorate it to your liking. Write the word "breathe" on it, for example, paint it with flowers or hearts, whatever you like yourself. Carry the pebble with you in your pocket and anytime you become aware of it or feel it in your pocket, take a minute or two to take some mindful breaths.

8. MINDFUL MOMENTS AND SOME LITTLE HELPERS

Mindful moments are basically mini meditations that can be done throughout the day without much preparation. Sometimes we just need little reminders and ideas to incorporate into our day. These mindful moments are suitable for us and our children and could consist of a mini body scan, a short breathing exercise or connecting to our senses (see mindful moment cards in the appendix). They are little helpers especially when we get a bit overwhelmed or need a little breather. These mindful moments just take a few minutes but can give us a real break to re-group and pull us out of our busy minds and into our bodies and the present moment.

Mindfulness wheel

Children sometimes need something to "grasp", a more tangible support. I adapted Daniel Siegel's "Wheel of Awareness" into a visual tool for children to tune into their senses, their interior world such as thoughts, their physical sensations and their connection to the world around them. Photocopy the wheel (see appendix) on cardboard. Children may want to colour it in and then assemble the wheel with the "hub" in the middle and an arrow to move around. Use a split pin to connect the parts so the arrow can move freely. Go through the wheel with your child the first couple of times to help them get used to the process.

Start the arrow at the senses and verbalise with them:

- "What do I hear?" – Pause for a minute and tune into the sounds around you.

- "What do I see?" – Pause for a minute and tune into your environment and what you can see.

- "What do I smell?" – Pause for a minute and become aware of any scents.

- "What tastes are in my mouth?" – Pause and focus on your sense of taste.

- "What sensations can I feel on my skin?" – Pause and pay attention to the sensations on your skin.

- Move the arrow to the next section of interior sensations.

- Move your attention inside your body.

- "Can I feel any tingling, discomfort, pain, tension, heat, movement, any other sensation?" – Stay with your attention on your body and become aware of the different parts of your body for a few minutes.

- Move the arrow over to the section of your mind, thoughts and emotions.

- "What am I thinking of?", "What emotions am I feeling at the moment?" Think of your mind as a blue sky with passing clouds (thoughts) or a guesthouse where everybody is welcome and will come and go when they're ready. You can just name or label them and let them go: "There's a worry; hello, jealousy; good morning, gratitude; bye-bye, anger."

- Now move your attention into the "hub" (picture child meditating on printable template in appendix) and try to include all of the different sections of awareness into "just awareness".

- This is the most abstract part for children and even us "grown-ups", and it takes quite a bit of practice. An important reminder is not to get frustrated. If your mind wanders and you notice it: that's awareness! Our minds will always be active, that's what minds do. Just direct attention back to your breathing again and again whenever it happens.

- Finally, move the arrow to the section of our exterior world: the people, the room, and the environment: all of our connections to the world.

- "Where am I?", "Who am I with?"

- You can extend your connection to wherever you like, even if it's to our planet Earth in general and its connections to other planets and the universe. We are all part of "the one".

- A daily practice of the wheel is basically a daily practice of mindfulness meditation. After a few trial runs children can do it independently, and you might just guide them towards a regular practice.

Mindfulness reminders

Children and adults can use mindfulness reminders, which can be anything we choose to remind us to have a little breather, to pay attention to the present moment, to be aware of the sensations in our bodies, to take a mindful pause and practise some mindful breathing. Mindful reminders could include a self-made bracelet, stickers placed in visible places such as on the fridge, laptop, iPad, front door or steering wheel. It could even be a little star drawn onto the back of our hand – anything that makes sense to you and catches your eye.

Body scan cards

This is a great activity for circle time in school or with your children at home. Photocopy the cards (see appendix) on firm cardboard and cut them out. Put them into a tin or a little bag. There are many variations for this activity. In a circle time one child could choose a card and all the children in the group focus their attention on this body part for a minute. The following example could be part of a morning routine at home or in school:

- Children can have their personal set of cards and pick three cards every morning or at the end of the day and direct their awareness into their body for a couple of minutes for each card. With a partner, children could instruct each other by taking turns choosing cards. There are many different possibilities.

9. GRATITUDE EXERCISES AND ACTIVITIES

Gratitude tree

This activity is lovely as a group exercise and display in a classroom, but it is also a great exercise for children at home and the whole family can get involved. Draw or paint a large bare tree together with the kids on a big piece of cardboard. Copy or draw leaves (can be green for spring and summer and colourful for autumn) and let children write down what they are grateful for. Stick the leaves on the tree for everybody to read. This is a lovely daily reminder of all the things we are grateful for.

Three things ...

This is a lovely exercise to include in your nightly bedtime routine. Maybe after reading a story take a couple of minutes for your child to think back on their day and pick three things that they are thankful for. It is a good idea to take turns with a parent, especially at the beginning when they may find this exercise a little difficult. With very young children you could start them off with just one thing and build it up from there. For older children the worksheet in the appendix could be coloured and laminated. You could use a journal, and every evening children could write down three things they are grateful for. After a while this exercise becomes part of a routine, not only of their day but most importantly of their minds. It will get easier and easier to identify things they are grateful for.

Gratitude alphabet

This is a nice exercise for circle time but can also be played as a family game around the dinner table. Taking turns and starting with the letter A, name things you are grateful for going through the letters of the alphabet.

Stop, smile and give thanks

This is more a little positive impulse that we can all integrate into any part of the day. It is literally just the intention to stop every so often during the day, take a few breaths and look around and just say thanks for whatever you notice in that moment. This could be anything at all, no matter how small. "Thank you for the sunshine," "thank you for my health" or "thank you for this lovely cup of tea" are just a few examples. The more we practise this, the more it becomes a natural behaviour that will occur more and more easily. Encourage your children to do the same and model it for them. This exercise will involuntarily help you to become more aware of your emotions, your blessings, your environment and the people within it, and it will integrate small nuggets of positivity that will spread more and more.

Gratitude charts and journals

For older children especially, it can be a nice "grounding" exercise to sit down and write down or draw what they are thankful for. Having a journal and every so often reading through it is also a nice way to remind ourselves of all the things that enrich our lives.

10. Mindful breaks for parents with their children

As I said in Part 1, we sometimes find it difficult to find enough space and time to share precious downtime with our children. Children crave physical and emotional connection to their parents, and it is crucial that we stop every so often to give this important feedback. It can be useful, especially in families that lead very busy lives, to intentionally set aside some time to spend with our children without any distractions. This does not necessarily have to involve formal mindfulness exercises; it could simply mean holding our child for five minutes while reading a story before bedtime. You can include mindful breathing while placing your hands on the child's belly or just enjoy a long hug. Taking regular parent–child time and making it a natural part of your daily routine enhances and supports connection and intimacy, and strengthens attachment, love and trust.

11. Exercises to identify and name emotions

Brainstorming exercises as group discussion

- "Name things that make you feel happy."
- "Name things that make you feel sad."
- "Name things that make you feel scared."
- "Name things that might hurt somebody else's feelings," etc.

Using metaphors and similes, such as colours, weather and animals, to identify emotions

This can be a great exercise for circle time. Sometimes it can be difficult and abstract for children to correctly identify their feelings and emotions. Metaphors and similes often make them more tangible for children to identify how they feel:

- "Today I feel a little stormy and rainy."
- "This morning I feel like a silly monkey."
- "I think I feel pretty yellow and pink today."

Make up your own metaphors. Children are very creative and open to these kinds of activities (see also weather badges in appendix).

"Face" exercises

On a blank face children draw how they feel at the moment (see worksheet). This exercise can be easily adapted to a cutting and gluing exercise depending on children's age and ability.

Feelings exercise

This relates to the story of a busy mind with different emotions like "fish in a pond". Draw faces for the fish showing the different emotions we can have and write down the emotion (see worksheets in appendix). This can be adapted to a cutting and gluing exercise depending on children's age and ability.

Variations include: birds or insects in the sky; clouds in the sky; mini beasts in a meadow and sea creatures in the sea.

12. EXERCISES TO NOTICE NEGATIVE FEELINGS/ EMOTIONS, NAME THEM AND LET THEM GO

Children understand abstract concepts more easily when they are explained in a multi-sensory or even just visual fashion. The physical "letting go" gives meaning to the concept and children are much more able to grasp what it means to let go of a feeling or emotion.

Flying balloons

Let children draw or write down feelings on a card. Attach the cards to a balloon and go outside to release the feelings and emotions. You can encourage the children to verbalise this action with a simple "bye-bye, anger", "farewell, sadness" etc.

Floating boats

Let children name negative emotions they might hold. They can either draw them or write them down on an A4 sheet of paper. Show them how to fold the paper into a little boat. Bring the children to a stream or pond where they can release their "emotion/feelings boat". Again encourage them to verbalise the letting go: "bye-bye for now, jealousy", "see you later, anger".

Flying planes

Exercise as above but then folded into paper planes. Find a suitable place outside on a height (e.g. unused bridge, fenced side of a hill, quarry, cliff or waterfall) and let them fly away. Try and find a place that enables the planes to disappear – you don't want the children getting frustrated that their planes don't fly far enough!

Posting letters

Again, let children write down or draw pictures of negative feelings/emotions they might hold at the moment. Seal the "letters" in an envelope and either let the children post them in a "home-made" letterbox or even in a real letterbox. Depending on the approach (confidential or open discussion) you decide what is appropriate and whether to "destroy" the evidence or to give them to the parents etc. The main focus is on the actual naming, recognising and letting go.

"Burning" negative feelings/emotions

This exercise is only suitable for outdoors and strictly supervised. Negative thoughts, feelings emotions are written down or drawn on a piece of paper and folded or scrunched up into a ball. Sitting around an open fire, children (and adults) wait their turn to throw their "bundle" into the fire and watch it burn and disappear in the flames. Obviously health and safety is of the highest priority.

Shaking, shouting, hopping, dancing, running and stamping out anger

Anger seems to be the emotion with the most obvious physical impact on children and can cause challenging behaviours such as lashing out, shouting, screaming, tantrums etc. Children have to know that it is okay to feel angry, but they also have to learn that it is not okay to hurt themselves or others as a reaction. Anger seems to build up a lot of physical tension and pressure. Rather than trying to contain this negative emotion, the most helpful way to deal with anger, especially in young children, is often giving them the opportunity to let it out with a physical activity. Depending on what is most appropriate and helpful in a certain situation, let them stamp it into the ground, punch it into a bean bag or boxing bag, dance or run it off, bounce it away in a trampoline, shout it into a room etc. When children are given the chance to relieve the physical pressure, it often is much easier to evaluate the situation afterwards and find meaningful solutions for a problem. The older and more mature children become, the more they will be able to find alternative coping strategies, such as expressing their anger verbally, writing it down or using an "angry squeezer" as my daughter calls it. This can be something like a rubber ball or a sand-filled balloon.

Emotions in our body

When we pay attention to it, we can feel the effects of our emotions in our body. I get cold hands and have to run to the toilet when I'm scared, my forehead becomes tense and I feel pressure on my eyes when I get worried and my throat constricts when I get angry or sad. These are a few personal examples of physical sensations caused by emotions. When children learn to notice where their emotions sit in their body and how they react to different emotions, it can greatly support them to "come back into their bodies" rather than getting carried away by anger, frustration or sadness etc. Regular "check-ins" or even short formal body scan meditations are a great way to remind children to bring awareness back into their bodies, which has an immediate calming effect especially when combined with mindful breathing. Another version of this exercise could be marking where they can feel certain emotions in their body on the included worksheet (see appendix). This could be an intervention in a situation where an emotion arises or a more general activity.

"The guest house exercise" based on this poem by Rumi:

The Guest House

This being human is a guest house.
Every morning a new arrival.

A joy, a depression, a meanness,
some momentary awareness comes
as an unexpected visitor.

Welcome and entertain them all!
Even if they are a crowd of sorrows,
who violently sweep your house
empty of its furniture,
still, treat each guest honourably.
He may be clearing you out
for some new delight.

The dark thought, the shame, the malice,
meet them at the door laughing
and invite them in.

Be grateful for whatever comes,
because each has been sent
as a guide from beyond.

— JALALUDDIN RUMI

This example can be used at home or in school. At circle time, for example, depending on the age group, either read the poem or tell a simplified version of it. Explain that we can see ourselves as this guest house, all guests are welcome, no matter who they are. They won't stay forever, they are only visitors who come and go again. There are many variations of activities. Children could be asked: "Who is visiting your guest house this morning?", "Have any visitors left already?" etc. You could use the template for children to draw their "visitors" or even have a large display on the wall where children can stick on/take off the different visiting guests every morning.

13. INDOOR MULTI-SENSORY ACTIVITIES

With all sensory activities, as well as any other activity, make sure the children will be able to take part and enjoy them. Find out beforehand if children have any allergies, sensitivities, likes and dislikes, fears or sensory integration difficulties. This ensures an enjoyable and fun experience as well as the building of trust and confidence.

Guess the picture (with a partner)

One person (A) sits comfortably with their back to their partner (parent/child). With their finger the other person (B) slowly draws a simple picture onto the back of their partner (e.g. sun, flower or apple). Now A has to guess what the picture is. Repeat for a couple of pictures then swap positions. This exercise requires trust (touch), but the tactile component can also be very enjoyable and relaxing. This activity promotes awareness and the experience of the present moment. This exercise can be changed to writing letters, numbers, words etc., whatever is appropriate for the developmental stage of the child.

Baking pizza

This is my eldest daughter's favourite part of our bedtime routine. One person (A) sits down in a comfortable position and closes his/her eyes. The partner (B) sits, stands or kneels behind A. In this activity, B pretends to bake a pizza on A's back. The process is acted out with hands on the back:

- "First I sprinkle the work surface with flour." (Tickle all ten fingers all across the back.)

- "Next I make a well in the middle and add salt, water and yeast." (Draw little circles in the middle of the back and tickle in the middle to add the ingredients.)

- "Next I start bringing in the flour to the middle and mix it with the other ingredients." (Stroking movements with both hands from outside to inside, then mixing motions.)

- "Now I need to knead the dough." (Massaging movements)

- "Next we start rolling it out." (With both hands flat on the back, move up and down, left and right.)

- "I get the tomato sauce ready and spoon some onto your pizza; spread it all over the pizza base." ("Blob" imaginary sauce with your hands and with flat hands spread it all over.)

- "Now I get your toppings and sprinkle them onto the tomato sauce."

- "Finally put your pizza into the oven and bake at a high heat." (Rub really fast with flat hands to create heat.)
- "Ready! Enjoy!"

This activity gives sensory stimulation, supports a story, helps awareness, builds trust and is fun! It can be adapted to all kinds of topics, such as "Safari through the jungle", "Planting seeds" and "Baking cookies". There's no end to the possibilities. Just adapt the language and actions to the children's developmental stage.

Leading you down the garden path

This exercise requires a little bit of preparation. It can be done outside or with a little bit of creativity inside as well. Create a barefoot path with different textures e.g. pebbles, sand, water, grass, straw, cloth etc. One partner has to take off their shoes and socks and is then blindfolded. The other person takes them by the hand and slowly leads them over the different textures. The blindfolded person then has to describe the different sensations. This exercise requires and builds trust, and there is heightened awareness of the senses due to the blindfolding.

Feelie bag

For this activity you need a soft cloth bag that can be accessed with both hands without the participating person being able to see what's inside. An easy way to make one is just tying a ribbon around the bottom part of a T-shirt and then using the two sleeves as entry points. It's a good idea to assemble a variety of objects with different shapes, sizes and textures and keep them in the bag so it can be used again and again. If you don't have a bag at hand just blindfold one participant. Person A selects an object and either places it in the bag to give to person B or places it in the hand of the blindfolded partner. They now have to inspect the object and guess what it is.

Tasting and smelling activities

It's always great fun to do blindfolded tasting and smelling activities. The blindfold really heightens the sense of taste and smell and makes the guessing very interesting. Like the raisin exercise, these activities help children understand the meaning of awareness. Again these activities require and build trust as well, and participants need to be mindful to make the experience a pleasant one (no chilli powder or mustard!). A good idea to make the smelling activities reusable is placing "smells" into photo-film canisters (if that's not a thing of the past!), and puncture the lid so they can be held up to your nose and release the scent.

The raisin exercise

This exercise is one of the first exercises in Jon Kabat-Zinn's meditation programme and is suitable for both adults and children. It can be a group activity or just an activity at home with your child. You can also use other foods if you think they are more suitable for your child. Sitting down comfortably, every participant gets a raisin and is asked to hold it in their hand for a minute. Then the participants are guided through the following steps:

1. **Holding**: First, take a raisin and hold it in the palm of your hand or between your finger and thumb.

2. **Seeing**: Take time to really focus on it; gaze at the raisin with care and full attention – imagine that you've just dropped in from Mars and have never seen an object like this before in your life. Let your eyes explore every part of it, examining the highlights where the light shines, the darker hollows, the folds and ridges and any asymmetries or unique features.

3. **Touching**: Turn the raisin over between your fingers, exploring its texture. Maybe do this with your eyes closed if that enhances your sense of touch.

4. **Smelling**: Hold the raisin beneath your nose. With each inhalation, take in any smell, aroma or fragrance that may arise. As you do this, notice anything interesting that may be happening in your mouth or stomach.

5. **Placing**: Now slowly bring the raisin up to your lips, noticing how your hand and arm know exactly how and where to position it. Gently place the raisin in your mouth; without chewing, notice how it gets into your

mouth in the first place. Spend a few moments focusing on the sensations of having it in your mouth, exploring it with your tongue.

6. **Tasting**: When you are ready, prepare to chew the raisin, noticing how and where it needs to be for chewing. Then, very consciously, take one or two bites into it and notice what happens in the aftermath, experiencing any waves of taste that emanate from it as you continue chewing. Without swallowing yet, notice the bare sensations of taste and texture in your mouth and how these may change over time, moment by moment. Also pay attention to any changes in the object itself.

7. **Swallowing**: When you feel ready to swallow the raisin, see if you can first detect the intention to swallow as it comes up, so that even this is experienced consciously before you actually swallow the raisin.

8. **Following**: Finally, see if you can feel what is left of the raisin moving down into your stomach, and sense how your body as a whole is feeling after you have completed this exercise.

Treasure chest

Fill a sizable box with rice, sand, wood shavings, muddy water, shaving foam or similar non-transparent material. "Hide" objects in the box and as a motivator maybe a treat as well. Blindfold the children and let them search for the hidden treasure with their hands. The different textures give sensory input; the activity of finding treasure is motivating and supports attention. Maybe integrate the activity into a story about a pirate treasure chest on an island or a sunken treasure in the sea. There are endless possibilities.

What's missing?

This activity can be done in groups or with one participant. For this game you need a variety of objects that you cover with a cloth before anybody can see them. The cloth is removed for a limited time (whatever seems appropriate for your age group) and the children are asked to memorise every object. When the time is up, children are asked to close their eyes and the parent or educator (or sibling, friend etc.) removes one or two of the objects. Participants can now open their eyes when prompted and have to guess which objects are missing. This game can be played with random objects or as part of a certain theme or topic, such as foods, vehicles, colours, shapes or animals etc. The aim of this activity is to focus the attention on what we see, taking in every detail for a limited amount of time and trying to memorise every object.

I spy with my little eye

This is an oldie but goldie and a mindfulness exercise we have all been doing for years! This game is a favourite in our family, especially on car journeys, and it really focuses the awareness of seeing. Depending on the age group you can use colour, shape, size or initial letters: I spy with my little eye something that is blue/round/big/beginning with "S".

Mindfulness bell

This is a great exercise to settle a class first thing in the morning but can be used in any setting, even by yourself. You can use a bell, gong, singing bowl, chime or even one of the widely available free apps. An extended ring would be recommended. Let children close their eyes and be very still. Before you ring the bell ask the children to listen very closely to the sound and instruct them to raise one arm when they cannot hear the ringing sound anymore but remain quiet until instructed to open their eyes.

14. ENVIRONMENTAL AWARENESS EXERCISES AND ACTIVITIES

Adventure/Nature boards/boxes

Every season and environment provides us with unique "gifts". Go outside! The great outdoors is an abundant source of possibilities to connect with our environment. To make outdoor trips exciting and interesting, gather little keepsakes and bring them home. Here you can recap on your adventure and remember what you saw and did. Be creative! Make a collage with seashells, sand, driftwood etc. to remember a beautiful day at the beach. In autumn, you can collect conkers, colourful leaves and acorns to create imaginative autumn creatures. With this type of exercise children can actively connect to nature and the seasons and get fully immersed in the experience. Always be respectful to nature and only collect items that won't "be missed".

Building a bird feeder

In the winter time birds often find it difficult to find food. With this activity children can gain a great sense of achievement and compassion towards other creatures. There are so many easy instructions for home-made birdfeeders available on the internet. It will be a fun art and craft activity as well as an act of kindness. When the feeders are put into place it is also a beautiful mindful activity to just watch the birds feeding, identify different colours or species or just even enjoy the spectacle.

Building an insect hotel

As above, building an insect hotel incorporates many different beneficial aspects. The process of making something with their own hands, feeling the textures and materials, learning about the importance of bees and other insects for nature and finally seeing their creation making a difference is a very satisfying process for children of all ages. After the insect hotel is installed, children can observe if and what type of hotel guests have moved in. Again there are a multitude of instructions for insect hotels to be found on the internet or in books and magazines. Be an architect and invent your own creation; there are no limits to creativity.

Brainstorming Display Board: how can we all make a difference?

As a feature either at home or in an educational setting, you could have a display board as a work in progress on which children can pin and express their ideas as to how they can make a difference, show initiative and present ideas about how they can help to be kind to their environment. Keep in mind not to confront young children with global challenges and keep lessons, conversations and impulses age appropriate, encouraging and positive. Try and implement children's ideas with them if you can, and encourage them to follow through with their initiatives. These could include:

- Collecting rubbish in the area where they live.
- Encouraging parents to use compostable bin bags.
- Cleaning up local eco-systems such as little streams or woodland.
- Reducing waste through mindful shopping.
- Installing a water filter rather than using bottled water.
- Saving energy in the house, i.e. switching off lights in rooms that aren't being used at that moment.

Children are creative and enthusiastic and with some guidance will come up with fantastic ideas!

Making craft projects from "rubbish"

Children learn in school about recycling and re-using, but the home is where they get a much better grasp of how they themselves can make a difference and instead of throwing everything away can re-use materials that would otherwise end up in the bin. There are endless art and craft projects; let children come up with their own ideas. A great starting point is having a couple of collection containers in which you can store different materials rather than throwing them in the bin. Collect plastic bottle tops, cardboard toilet or kitchen towel rolls, empty containers and boxes, flattened cereal boxes. I know sometimes we are stuck for space, so adapt to your own situations and even ask local schools, childcare centres and art classes if they are interested in these materials. Drop them off with your children so they can see materials can be re-used.

15. STORYTELLING

Stories told by parents, grandparents or other close friends and family have been an integral part of bonding and sharing special quality time together for centuries. Stories can be used for so many reasons: they can help to identify and explain emotions, teach about kindness and compassion, help to understand difficult concepts, encourage imagination and creativity, transport us into a magical imaginary world, help us relax or simply take us on an enjoyable journey.

It can be difficult to explain abstract concepts in simple words especially to young children. Rather than trying to "just" describe and explain, it is usually much easier, more appropriate and fun to tell a story that children are motivated by and can relate to. These could be "self-composed" or chosen from a book. Children usually love a good story, and they can get fully immersed in an imaginary world created by the tale. I really like the following example of Dr Amy Saltzman of introducing mindfulness to children:

> Hello. My name is Amy, and I would like to share one of my favourite places with you. I call it Still Quiet Place. It's not a place you travel to in a car, or a train, or a plane. It is a place inside you that you can find just by closing your eyes. Let's find it now.
>
> Close your eyes and take some slow deep breaths. See if you can feel a kind of warm, happy smile in your body. Do you feel it? This is your Still Quiet Place. Take some more deep breaths and really snuggle in.
>
> The best thing about your Still Quiet Place is that it's always inside you. And you can visit it whenever you like. It is nice to visit your Still Quiet Place and feel the love that is there. It is especially helpful to visit your Still Quiet Place if you are feeling angry, or sad, or afraid. The Still Quiet Place is a good place to talk with these feelings and to make friends with them. When you rest in your Still Quiet Place and talk to your feelings, you may find that your feelings are not as big and as powerful as they seem. Remember, you can come here whenever you want, and stay as long as you like.

Susan Kaiser Greenland adds that storytelling can be used effectively when practising and teaching mindfulness to young children:

> There are stories that transcend time, place, language and culture. Well-told tales serve to model positive social qualities that lead to healthy relationships, psychological freedom, and happiness. When practising with your kids, remember to draw from fables and stories from your own childhood, and make up your own too.

One of my fondest memories of my early childhood is hopping into my parents' bed on a Sunday morning and my dad telling us stories, mainly Aesop's fables such as "The Fox and the Raven" or "The Hare and the Tortoise". They were short but poignant tales conveying valuable messages, and I still recall most of them.

In the following section of resources you will find an extensive list of children's books that you might find beneficial for your children or work in school.

16. MANDALA ACTIVITIES

There are lots of printable mandala templates available either in books or on the internet. I have included a template in the appendix to help you create your own mandala, but I will leave it up to you to find suitable mandalas should you like to use some at home or in an educational setting. I just want to give some ideas as to how creating mandalas can be included in outdoor play or art and craft activities using various materials. As described previously, mandalas don't necessarily have to be on paper. Any background, surface or material can become a mandala; the possibilities are endless:

Pebble, seashell, seaweed, driftwood, sea glass mandala

Acorn, leaf, twig, nut mandala

Flower and blossom mandala

Fruit and vegetable mandala

Mandala collage using cut-outs from magazines etc.

Potato stamp mandala using various shapes

Sand mandala

Treat mandala for a party (i.e. jellies, chocolates, biscuits etc.)

Rubbish recycling mandala

Mandala made from pasta shapes, seeds, rice.

Resources

————

There is a vast amount of books on meditation and, in particular, mindfulness meditation on the market. The following is my own personal "bestseller list" of books about mindfulness in general as well as those specifically related to parenting and education. I have found them hugely beneficial for writing this book as well as for my personal mindfulness and parenting/teaching journey to date. This list is by no means comprehensive, and I know there is a multitude of very worthwhile books out there, many of which I am hoping to read in the future.

Mindfulness-based books for further reading:

- *Brainstorm, The Power and Purpose of the Teenage Brain*, Daniel J. Siegel
- *Calming your Anxious Mind*, Jeffrey Brantley
- *Calm Kids*, Lorraine E. Murray
- *Child's Mind*, Christopher Willard
- *Everyday Blessings*, Myla and Jon Kabat-Zinn
- *Freedom in Exile*, His Holiness the Dalai Lama
- *Full Catastrophe Living*, Jon Kabat-Zinn
- *Happier*, Tal Ben-Shahar
- *Into The Magic Shop*, James Doty
- *Loving Kindness – The Revolutionary Art of Happiness*, Sharon Salzberg
- *Mindfulness – A Practical Guide to Finding Peace in a Frantic World*, Mark Williams & Danny Penman

- *Mindful Teaching and Teaching Mindfulness*, Deborah Schoeberlein
- *Mindsight*, Daniel J. Siegel
- *Parenting from the Inside Out*, Daniel J. Siegel & Mary Hartzell
- *Peace Is Every Step*, Thich Nhat Hanh
- *Planting Seeds – Practicing Mindfulness With Children*, Thich Nhat Hanh
- *Reconciliation*, Thich Nhat Hanh
- *The Art of Meditation*, Matthieu Ricard
- *The Brain's Way of Healing*, Norman Doidge
- *The Mindful Brain*, Daniel J. Siegel
- *The Mindful Child*, Susan Kaiser Greenland
- *The Way of Mindful Education*, Daniel Rechtschaffen
- *When Things Fall Apart*, Pema Chodron
- *Wherever You Go, There You Are*, Jon Kabat-Zinn

Books for children:

I have compiled the following book list of mindfulness literature for children. They touch on various topics, including kindness and compassion, gratitude, feelings and guided mindfulness stories. You might like to use them at home, in school or in other settings. You know your children or the children you work with best and can choose whatever is appropriate for their age, personality, setting and situation.

- *A Boy and a Turtle*, Lori Lite
- *A Chair for my Mother*, Vera B. Williams
- *Affirmation Weaver*, Lori Lite
- *Anh's Anger*, Gail Silver, Christiane Kromer
- *A Nifflenoo called Nevermind*, Margot Sunderland, Nicky Hancock

- *A Sick Day for Amos McGee*, Philip C. Stead & Erin E. Stead

- *Each Kindness*, Jacqueline Woodson

- *Enemy Pie*, Derek Munson

- *Good-Bye Bumps! – Talking To What's Bugging You*, Dr Wayne W. Dyer, Saje Dyer

- *How Hattie hated Kindness*, Margot Sunderland, Nicky Hancock

- *Horton Hears a Who?*, Dr Seuss

- *I Am: Why Two Little Words Mean so Much*, Dr Wayne W. Dyer with Kristina Tracy

- *Incredible You!*, Dr Wayne W. Dyer with Kristina Tracy

- *I think, I Am!*, Louise Hay, Kristina Tracy

- *Just Me and My Mind*, Kerry Lee MacLean

- *Last Stop on Market Street*, Matt de la Pena

- *Meditation is an Open Sky*, Whitney Stewart

- *No Excuses! How What You Say can get in Your Way*, Dr Wayne W. Dyer, Kristina Tracy

- *No Ordinary Apple*, Sara Marlowe

- *Ordinary Mary's Extraordinary Deed*, Emily Pearson

- *Peace, Bugs and Understanding*, Gail Silver

- *Please Explain "Anxiety" to Me!*, Laurie Zelinger, Ph.D., Jordan Zelinger, MS Ed.

- *Rude Cakes*, Rowboat Watkins

- *Sam and the Lucky Money*, Karen Chinn

- *Sea Otter Cove*, Lori Lite

- *Starfish On The Beach*, Lindy and Tom Schneider

- *Steps and Stones*, Gail Silver, Christiane Kroemer

- *Take the Time: Mindfulness for Kids*, Maud Roegiers

- *The Frog that Longed for the Moon to Smile*, Margot Sunderland, Nicky Hancock
- *The Giving Tree*, Shel Silverstein
- *The Invisible Boy*, Trudy Ludwig
- *The Listening Walk*, Paul Showers
- *The Smartest Giant in Town*, Julia Donaldson
- *The Tree Questions*, Jon J. Muth
- *Thinking Stories to Wake up your Mind*, Mike Fleetham
- *Those Shoes*, Maribeth Boelts
- *Tiger-Tiger is it True?*, Byron Katie, Hans Wilhelm
- *Tight Times*, Barbara Shook Hazen
- *Unstoppable Me! 10 Ways to Soar Through Life*, Dr Wayne W. Dyer, Kristina Tracy
- *Visiting Feelings*, Lauren Rubenstein
- *We all Sing with the Same Voice*, J. Philip Miller & Sheppard M. Greene
- *Willy and the Wobbly House*, Margot Sunderland, Nicky Hancock
- *Your Fantastic Elastic Brain*, Joann Deak Ph.D.
- *Zen Ties*, John J. Muth

Useful websites and apps:

Again, these are websites and apps that I personally frequent and use. I am sure there are many other beneficial websites and apps out there.

Websites:

www.atlasofemotions.org
www.blissfulkids.com
www.greatergood.berkeley.edu
www.cw.uhs.harvard.edu
www.mindfulnesscds.com

www.mindfulnessmatters.ie
www.mindfulschools.org
www.relaxkids.com
www.mindup.org/thehawnfoundation/

Apps:

Jkz Series 1, Jon Kabat-Zinn
Jkz Series 2, Jon Kabat-Zinn
Jkz Series 3, Jon Kabat-Zinn
Mindfulness and Psychotherapy, Thich Nhat Hanh
Mindfulness for Beginners, Jon Kabat-Zinn
Plum Village Meditations, Thich Nhat Hanh

CDs and books with formal meditation exercises for children:

CDs:

Indigo Dreams Series, Lori Lite
Mindfulness Matters, "The Zone"
Mindfulness Matters, "Still Space"
Mindfulness Matters, "Sleep" for kids
Still and quiet space, Amy Saltzman

Books:

Aladdin's Magic Carpet, Marneta Viegas
A Still Quiet Place, Amy Saltzman
Little Book of Stars, Marneta Viegas
MindUP Curriculum, The Hawn Foundation
Sitting Still like a Frog, Eline Snel
The Magic Box, Marneta Viegas
The Mindful Child, Susan Kaiser Greenland
The Wishing Star, Marneta Viegas

Bibliography

Alidina, S. (2010) *Mindfulness for Dummies*. Chichester, John Wiley and Sons Ltd.

Asmussen, Dan, untitled story on his facebook page on 21.07.2015.

Anthony, David W. (1996) Bridling Horsepower: The Domestication of the Horse. In Olsen, S.L. (1996) *Horses through Time*. Pittsburgh, Roberts Rinehart Publishers.

Ayres, A.J. (1979) *Sensory Integration and the Child*. Los Angeles, Western Psychological Services.

Ball, P. (2010) *The Music Instinct*. London, The Bodley Head.

Ben-Shahar, T. (2008) *Happier*. Maidenhead, McGraw-Hill Publishing Company.

Bergstrom, C. (2016) The Mindful Brain – Mindfulness and the brain – How to explain it to children. http://blissfulkids.com/mindfulness-and-the-brain-how-to-explain-it-to-children/

Bersma, D., Visscher, M. (2003) *Yoga Games for Children*. Alameda, Hunter House Inc.

Berry, L., Poem "The Last Time" (unpublished) http://www.lucyberry.com/

Biel, L.; Peske, N. (2009) Raising a Sensory Smart Child. London, Penguin Books Ltd.

Black, D.S. Mindfulness Research Guide – A new Paradigm for managing empirical health information. Mindfulness, 1(3), 174 (2010)

Bondavalli, M., Mori, M. and Vecchi, V. (Eds) and Children of Reggio Emilia (1993) Children in Reggio Emilia look at the School Children's Environments, 10 (2) 39–45. http://www.jstor.org/journal/chilyoutenvi

Brensilver, M. (2016) What is Mindfulness? http://www.mindfulschools.org/foundational-concepts/what-is-mindfulness/

Brown, D. (2016) *Happy*. London, Transworld Publishers.

Brown, Mac H. and Freeman, N.K. (2001) "We don't play that way at preschool": the moral and ethical dimensions of controlling children's play, in S. Reifel and Mac H. Brown (Eds) Early Education and Care and Reconceptualising Play – Advances in Early Education and Day Care, Volume II (Oxford, Elsevier Science), 259–74.

Brownn, E. (2014) www.eleanorbrownn.com

Bruner, J.S. (1972) Nature and uses of immaturity. American Psychologist, 27, 687–708.

Burdick, D. (2014) *Mindfulness Skills for Kids and Teens*. Eau Claire, PESI Publishing & Media.

Butler, P. (2016) No grammar schools, lots of play: the secrets of Europe's top education system. http://www.theguardian.com/education/2016/sep/20/grammar-schools-play-europe-top-education-system-finland-daycare

Chamberlin, J.E. (2007) *Horse – How the horse has shaped Civilisation*. Canada, Vintage Canada.

Cooper, H. (2006) Homework helps students succeed in school, as long as there isn't too much. https://today.duke/edu/2006/03/homework/html

Doty, J.R. (2016) *Into the Magic Shop*. London, Yellow Kite.

Einarsdottir, J. (2005) We can decide what to play! Children's perception of quality in an Icelandic playschool. Early Education and Development, 16 (4), 470–88.

Ekman, P. (2015) "What scientists who study emotions agree on." www.paulekman.com

Elkind, D. (2007) *The Hurried Child: growing up too fast too soon*. 25th Anniversary edition. New York, Da Capo Lifelong Learning.

Elkind, D. (2007) *The Power of Play – Learning what comes naturally*. New York, Da Capo Press.

Field, T. (2001) *Touch*. The MIT Press.

Fincher, S.F. (2010) *Creating Mandalas*. Boston, Shambhala Publications, Inc.

Finnish National Agency for Education, www.oph.fi

Gehart, D.R. (2012) *Mindfulness and Acceptance in Couple and Family Therapy*. New York, Springer Science and Business Media.

Government of Ireland (1999) Primary School Curriculum – Art Education–Music. Dublin, The Stationery Office.

Grandin, T. (1992) Calming effects of Deep Touch Pressure in Patients with Autistic Disorder, College Students, and Animals. Journal of Child and Adolescent and Psychopharmacology, Vol. 2, Nr.1, Mary Ann Liebert Inc. Publishers.

Grandin, T. and Johnson, C. (2005) *Animals in Translation*. London, Bloomsbury Publishing Plc.

Grobler, R. (2004) *The Influence of Therapeutic Horseriding on Neuropsychological Outcomes on Children with Tourette's Syndrome*. Pretoria, Faculty of Humanities, University of Pretoria.

Gross, J.J. (ed.) (2014) *Handbook of emotion regulation*. New York, Guilford Press.

Gross, J.J. and Thompson, R. (2007). *Emotion Regulation: Conceptual Foundations. Handbook of Emotion Regulation*. 3-27.

Happiness is, Andrew Shapter, dir. (Faron West Productions, 2009) [documentary film].

Kabat-Zinn, M. and Kabat-Zinn, J. (1997) *Everyday Blessings – The Inner Work of Mindful Parenting*. New York, Hyperion.

Kernan, M. (2007) Play as a context for Early Learning and Development – A research paper. Dublin, NCCA.

Kaiser Greenland, S. (2010) *The Mindful Child*. New York, Atria Paperback.

LeTendre, G.K. (2015) Does homework help or hinder young children? http://www.independent.co.uk/life-style/health-and-families/ does-homework-help-or-hinder-young-children-10484928.html

LeFebvre, J.E. (2009) *Parenting the Pre-Schooler*. Eagle River, University of Wisconsin.

Louv, R. (2005) *Last Child in the Woods*. New York, Alonquin Books of Chapel Hill.

Malloch, S. (2005) Why do we love to dance and sing? In: Grove, R., Stevens, C., and McKechnie, S. (eds.), *Thinking in Four Dimensions: Creativity and Cognition in Contemporary Dance*. Melbourne University Press.

Malchiodi, C.A, (1998) *Understanding Children's Drawings*. New York, The Guilford Press.

Margalit, L. (2016) What Screen Time Can Really do to Kids' Brains. https://www.psychologytoday.com/blog/behind-online-behavior/201604/what-screen-time-can-really-do-kids-brains

Neff, K.D. (2009) The Role of Self-Compassion in Development: A Healthier Way to Relate to Oneself. Human Development 2009; 52; 211–14, DOI 10.1159/000215071.

Neff, K.D. and McGehee, P. (in press). Self-compassion and psychological resilience among adolescents and young adults. Self and identity.

Neff, K.D. (2017) What is Self-Compassion? http://self-compassion. org/the-three-elements-of-self-compassion-2/

Neihardt, J. (ed.). (1961) *Black Elk Speaks*. Lincoln, University of Nebraska Press.

Obert, M. (2012) Zwischen Hoelle und Hoffnung. Sueddeutsche Zeitung Nr.16/2012.

Parker, K, van Wieren, G. (2014) Playing Outside could make Kids more Spiritual. http://msutoday.msu.edu/news/2014/playing-outside-could-make-kids-more-spiritual/

Payne, K.J. and Ross, L.M. (2009) *Simplicity Parenting – Using the Extraordinary Power of Less to raise Calmer, Happier and More Secure Kids*. New York, Ballantine Books.

Pedersen, T. (2014) Playing Outside Nurtures Spirituality in Children. http://spiritualityhealth.com/blog/traci-pedersen/playing-outside-nurtures-spirituality-children

Reilly, K. (2016) Is homework good for kids? Here is what the research says. www.time.com/4466390/homework-debate-research

Reimer, B. (2005) *New Brain Research on Emotion and Feeling: Dramatic Implications for Music Education.* Washington, Heldref Publications.

Renz-Polster, H., Huether, G. (2013) *Wie Kinder heute wachsen.* Weinheim und Basel, Beltz Verlag.

Roeper, M. (2011) *Kinder raus!* Muenchen, Suedwest Verlag.

Saltzman, A. (2004, in press) *A Still Quiet Place: Manual for teaching mindfulness-based stress reduction to children.* Will be available in the context of workshops and trainings through www.stillquietplace.com.

Seligman, M. (2003) *Authentic Happiness.* London, Nicholas Brealey Publishing.

Seligman, M. (2013) *Flourish.* New York, Simon & Schuster Inc.

Siegel, D., Hartzell, M. (2014) *Parenting from the Inside Out.* London, Scribe Publications.

Siegel, D. (2015) *No Drama Discipline.* London, Scribe Publications.

Siegel, D. (2014) *Brainstorm.* London, Scribe Publications.

Siegel, D. (2010) *Mindsight: Transform Your Brain with the New Science of Kindness.* New York, Bantam Books.

Siegel, D., Payne Bryson, T. (2012) *The Whole-Brain Child.* New York, Bantam Books.

Snel, E. (2013) *Sitting still like a Frog.* Boston, Shambala Publications.

Spicer, S. (2007) The Importance of Touch - From hugs to high-fives, kids of all ages need to physically feel our love. https://www.todaysparent.com/family/the-importance-of-touch/

Sutton, C. (2012) 8-week Mindfulness Programme with Catherine Sutton MA in Mindfulness-Based Approaches. Lismore, self-published booklet.

Taylor, J. (2012) Is our survival instinct failing us? https://www. psychologytoday.com/blog/the-power-prime/201206/is-our-survival-instinct-failing-us

Twenge, J.M. and Campbell, W.K. (2009) *The Narcissism Epidemic.* New York, Atria Paperback.

UNESCO, www.unesco.org

Ungar, M. (2009) *The We Generation – Raising Socially Responsible Kids.* Halifax, Da Capo Press.

Vallatton, C. and Ayoub, C. (2011) Use Your Words: The role of language in the development of toddlers' self-regulation. Early Childhood Research Quarterly.

Van Wieren, G. and Parker, K. (2014) Playing Outside Could Make our Kids more Spiritual. http://msutoday.msu.edu/news/2014/playing-outside-could-make-kids-more-spiritual/

Vatterott, C. (2009) *Rethinking Homework.* Alexandria, ASCD.

Violatti, C. (2013) Definition Mandala. http://www.ancient.eu/mandala/

Vygotsky, L. S. (1978) The Role of Play in Development. In Mind in Society. (pp. 92–104). Cambridge, MA: Harvard University Press.

Whitebread, D. (2011) *Developmental Psychology and Early Childhood Education.* London, Sage.

Whitfield, C.L. (1987) *Healing the Child Within.* Deerfield Beach, Health Communications Inc.

Whitebread, D. (2012) *The Importance of Play, a report on the value of children's play with a series of policy recommendations.* University of Cambridge.

Wiking, M. (2016) *The Little Book of Hygge.* Penguin Life.

Acknowledgements

There are many people I want to thank for their support. Chenile Keogh, Maria McGuinness, Robert Doran at Kazoo Independent Publishing Services for their fantastic support and professional input, Andrew Brown at Ardel Media for the great cover design, Cathy Dineen for the beautiful artwork, Berit Alits for letting me use some of the treasured photographs she took for us, Joe Kenny for rescuing my computer multiple times and being the number one IT support, this book mightn't have made it without you, all the amazing authors who let me share some of their incredible knowledge and wisdom. Thank you! Last but not least thank you to my wonderful husband Michael and my two daughters Julianna and Jona for giving me the support and freedom to do this project, for your love and patience and for being the inspiration for this book.

Appendix

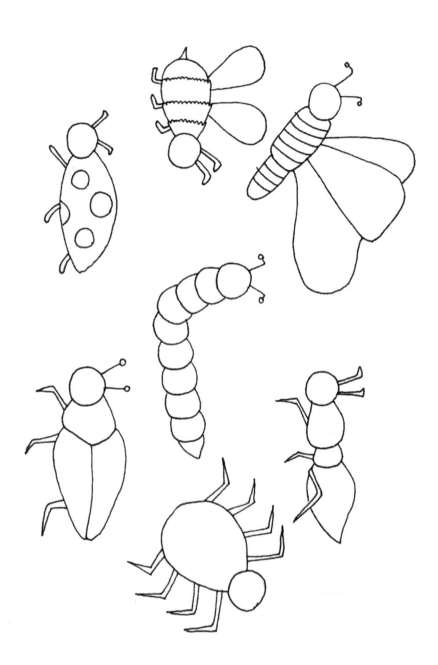

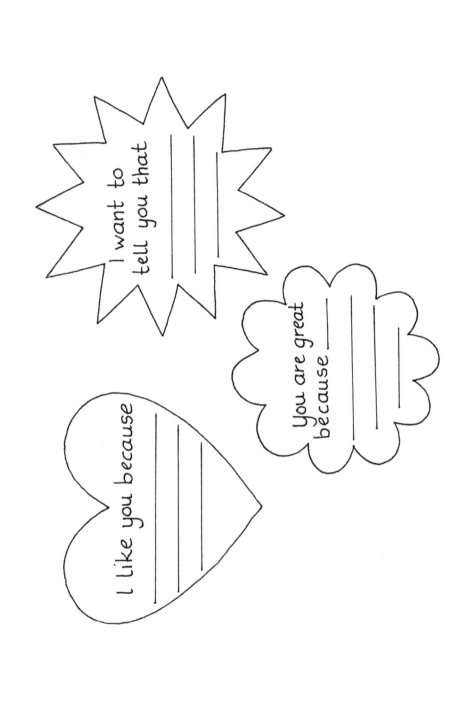

Kindness Challenge: This week I will...

Name:

Date:

...share something.

...tidy up my room without being asked.

...write a letter to someone.

...smile at people.

...help with chores.

...sort out some toys for children who don't have as many.

...give more hugs.

...visit somebody who might feel lonely.

...give somebody an unexpected gift.

The Star Thrower

A man was walking on the beach one day and noticed a boy who
was reaching down, picking up a starfish and throwing it in
the ocean. As he approached he called out, "Hello! What are you
doing?" The boy looked up and said, " I'm throwing starfish into
the ocean." "Why are you throwing starfish into the ocean?"
asked the man. "The tide stranded them. If I don't throw them
into the water before the sun comes up, they'll die," came the
answer. "Surely you realise that there are miles of beach, and
thousands of starfish. You'll never throw them all back, there are
too many. You can't possibly make a difference." The boy listened
politely, then picked up another starfish. As he threw it back into
the sea, he said, "It made a difference to this one."

(based on the essay "The Star Thrower' by Loren Eisely 1969)

Body scan cards:

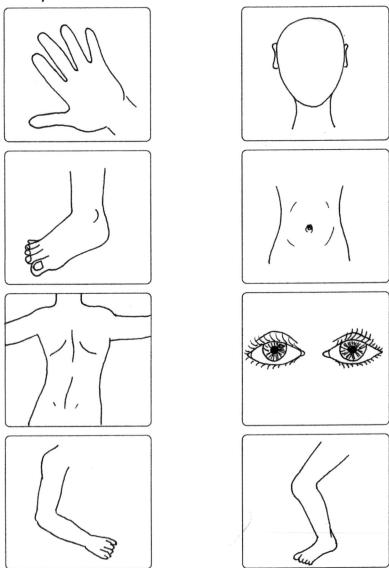

Body scan cards:

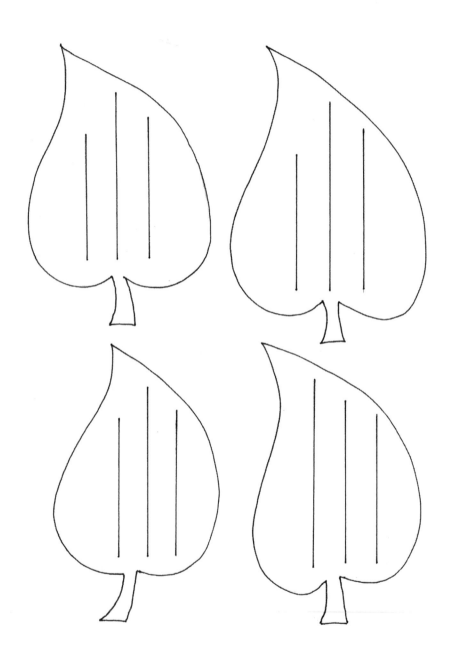

for _____

for _____

for _____

I am grateful

3 good things
about my day

⭐ I really enjoyed _____

⭐ _____

⭐ My favourite _____

⭐ _____

⭐ I loved _____

⭐ _____

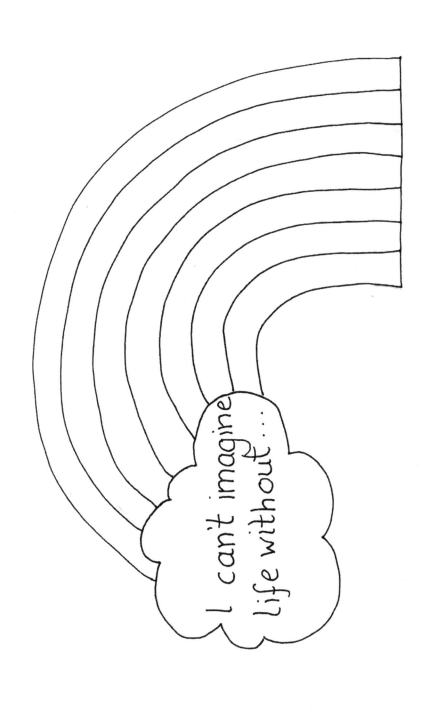

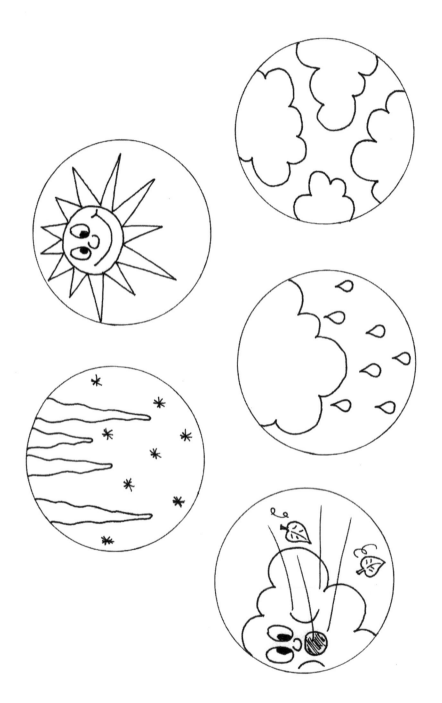

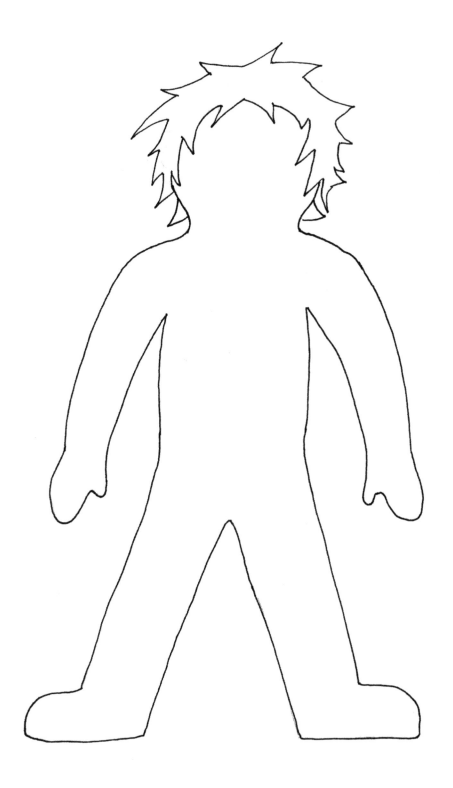

The Guest House

Adapted version for children from "The Guest House" by Jellaludin Rumi (original)

Our minds are like a guest house.
Every day we welcome new visitors.

Happiness, sadness, anger,
Some feelings and emotions,
Can be unexpected guests.

Welcome and embrace them all!
Even if they are a little frightening or unpleasant,
Sometimes sweeping in like a storm,
Messing up the house,
Still, treat them all well,
Maybe a good clean-up
Can make room for something new and beautiful.

The worrying thought, the shame, the jealousy,
Meet them all at the door laughing and invite them in.

Be grateful for whatever comes.
Because each guest has been sent,
For a reason.

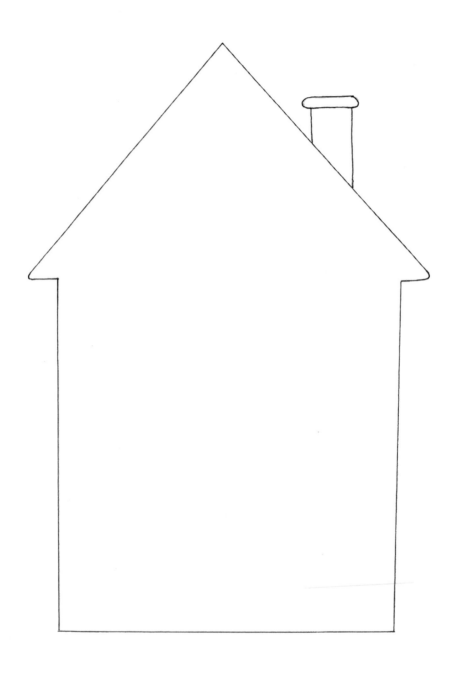

Mindful Moment Cards:

In the evening sit down and take a few mindful breaths. Recap your day and write down three positive things that happened during the day. Place the dated note into a "Happy Jar". At the end of the year, pick out some notes and remember.

For the next twenty steps, slow down and feel your feet touching the earth. Become aware of your feet, yourself, connecting with our planet.

Close your eyes and place your hand on your heart. Take some mindful breaths and connect to your heart. Say quietly or out loud:
May I be happy and well.
May I be healthy and whole.
May I be free from pain.
May I live with ease and joy.

Place your awareness on your thoughts with an open mind. Think of your mind as a guesthouse, everybody (all of your thoughts) is welcome, guests can stay a while and then they leave again. You can even verbalise to yourself: "Hello worry, see you later judgement."

Mindful Moment Cards:

Stop and look around you. Find three things that you hadn't noticed up to now. Look at them closely: what colour are they, what shape, what size?

When out for a walk give thanks for three things you notice around you. Really see them and say to yourself or out loud:
Thank you for the tree.
Thank you for the sun.
Thank you for the birdsong.

Put your hands on your tummy and feel it rising and falling with every breath. Count ten breaths, breathing in and ten breaths breathing out; become aware of where you can feel your breath coming in and out.

Stop for a moment, close your eyes and just listen. What can you hear? Are there nature sounds, passing cars, people chatting?

Mindful Moment Cards:

Sitting or standing, notice what you touch or what you are touched by. Feel the ground under your feet, the surface you are sitting on, the texture of your clothes, shoes, wath, jewellery etc.

Life in slow motion: Just for a few minutes slow yourself down. Walk and move slowly, notice what you are doing, notice where you are and who you are with. Notice how you are feeling, what you are thinking. Taking some "slow motion" minutes will pull you back into the present moment.

Write down three things that make you happy. Connect to this feeling of happiness and really let it into your body and mind. "Bathe" in this feeling for a few minutes.

Think of three people, one you love, one you feel neutral about, one you have a difficult relationship with. Connect to your heart and send a kind message to each of them. Finally send a kind message to yourself.

Mindful Moment Cards:

Give someone you love a twenty-second-hug. A long hug releases the bounding hormone oxytocin which lowers anxiety and supports general well-being.

Cycle of the senses. Tune into each of your senses for a minute. What can you see? What can you hear, taste, smell in this moment? What sensations can you feel on your skin? Can you feel any tension or tingling in your body? Do some stretches to release discomfort.

Put on your favourite dancing song. Dance, jump, bounce, wriggle, shake, sway out all of your tension, maybe anger, frustration, or just enjoy the feeling of your body moving to the music.

Mindful eating. Really pay attention to your food. See what it looks like, feel its texture and temperature. Is it sweet or savoury? Smell its aromas. Really taste the food with awareness and presence.

Mindful Moment Cards:

Connect to nature. Step outside, close your eyes and breathe, becoming aware of the breeze, the scents, the sounds. Open your eyes and observe nature, the flowers and trees, the birds and insects. Feel your connection to nature and the earth.

Mini Body scan:
Move your awareness slowly through your body from your crown to face, neck, throat, shoulders, arms, hands, chest, belly, hips and buttocks, thighs, knees, calves and feet. Can you feel any tension or tingling? Relax and release the tension with some stretches.

Close your eyes and "look at your eyes from the inside". Become aware of your eyelids and your eyes behind them.
Stay with this awareness for two or three minutes.

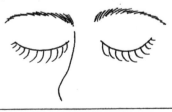

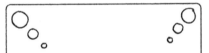

Take a deep breath into your belly and breathe out with your lips making an extended "mmmmmmmm" sound.
Repeat for a few breaths.

Mindful Moment Cards:

Get yourself a treat, a bar of chocolate, a piece of fruit, a nice drink. Sit down and really enjoy this treat, taste it, savour it, experience it with all your senses, take some "me time".

When you're experiencing a difficult emotion like anger, jealousy or sadness, try and investigate:
Where can I feel it in my body? What does it feel like? Does it have a colour or shape? Embrace it, what does it want to tell you? What do you need?

Give yourself a hug. See yourself as your best friend. Tell yourself that you are here for you and that you love yourself. Even if it feels odd at first, connect to your heart and say out loud:
"I love myself. I am perfect, just the way I am."

You are a tree. Stand in a stable position "rooting" yourself. Stand tall and upright imagining you are a tree. Strong and tall, firmly anchored to the earth. Breathe and feel this connection for a few minutes.

Blank Mandala Template:

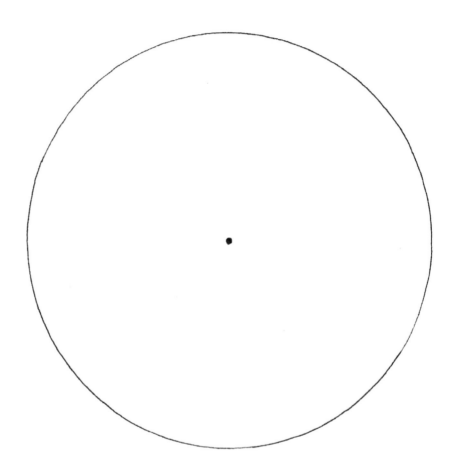

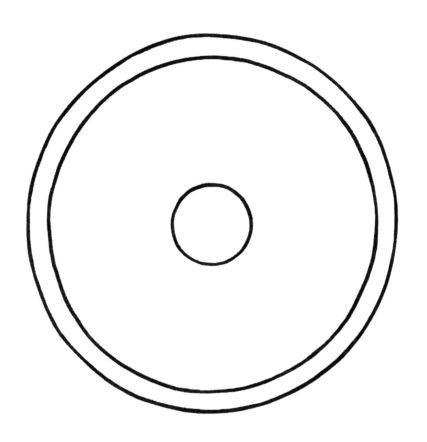

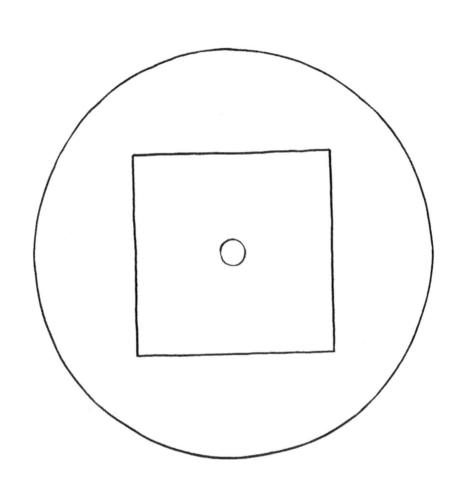

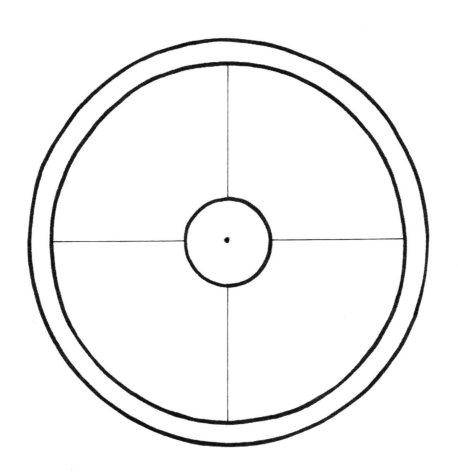